Dog Problems
The Gentle Modern Cure

Dog Problems
The Gentle Modern Cure

David Weston & Ruth Ross

HOWELL
BOOK HOUSE
New York

Howell Book House
A Simon & Schuster Macmillan Company
1633 Broadway
New York, NY 10019

Printed in Hong Kong

Library of Congress Cataloging-in-Publication Data

Weston, David, 1929–
    Dog problems: the gentle modern cure / David Weston & Ruth Ross
       p. cm.
    ISBN 0-87605-507-2
    1. Dogs—Training. 2. Dogs—Behavior. I. Ross, Ruth (Elizabeth Ruth). II. Title.
SF431.W46   1993   93-13559   CIP
636.7′0887—dc20

10 9 8 7

CONTENTS

ACKNOWLEDGEMENTS

We have drawn on the knowledge and expertise of many scientists in order to write this book:

We wish to acknowledge the work of the early twentieth century physiologist, Ivan Pavlov, who inadvertently discovered one of the learning processes which has become known as classical conditioning.

The late Burrhus Skinner, a Harvard psychologist, continued the pioneering work of Edward Thorndike and John Watson, and dedicated his life to the study of another learning process which he called operant conditioning. The process emphasised the power of reinforcement as a means of influencing behaviour.

Present-day psychologists John Scott and John Fuller undertook a twenty-year research project studying and categorising dog behaviour. Amongst other things, their scientific data proved that there is a critical period for socialising dogs during their early development which is of great significance to all dog owners.

The observations of wolf biologist David Mech, and other scientists who have studied wolf behaviour in the wild, helped us to compare wolf and dog behaviour and to determine what is natural, and what behaviours we have modified by domestication.

Monty Sloan of Wolf Park, RR1, Battle Ground, Indiana 47920, USA, was kind enough to supply us with the slides of the wolf which appear in this book. He is the production editor of *Wolf!*, an independent quarterly magazine which is dedicated to wolf survival in the wild and to its welfare in captivity.

We also wish to thank the friends who have helped us with this book: Val Hobson who typed the first and second draft of the manuscript, Judy Addison and Elaine Stewart who lent us their beach home 'Wendover' where much of the brainstorming was done, and Anne Godden whose editorial skills were invaluable and who stopped us from falling into the trap of using too much jargon.

Our gratitude also goes to the dogs and dog owners who gave up their time to be photographed and to all the instructors, committee and members of The Kintala Club who have helped to spread the word about the method of training which David started developing twenty years ago. It is not always easy to be part of an organisation whose methods and philosophy diverge so markedly from traditional mainstream thinking. New knowledge is often hard to accept!

David Weston and Ruth Ross
May 1992

CHAPTER 1 MAN'S BEST FRIEND — A WOLF?!

Pets play an important part in the lives of many people and a high percentage of households in most industrialised countries own either a dog, or cat, or both. Unfortunately, statistics show that hundreds of thousands of these animals end up being put to death each year. The reason that most dogs finish up their lives in this unfortunate way is because they develop behavioural problems which their owners are not willing or able to cope with.

We all have great expectations of how our dogs should behave! But when our dogs develop a 'problem', do we ever ask ourselves if they are really just showing a part of normal dog behaviour which has only become a problem because the dog has to fit into our lifestyle? After all, if we didn't have all the trappings of modern civilisation like cars, houses, furniture, washing, gardens and other domesticated animals, our dogs couldn't chase cars, urinate in the house, pull washing off the line, dig holes and uproot our favourite plants or chase the neighbour's cat!

So what can we do about it? Obviously, if we choose to share our life with one or more dogs, then the dogs' behaviour must be acceptable to us, our friends, neighbours and veterinarian. But this shouldn't be a one-way affair. It's not just up to the dog to modify its actions so that we can live together successfully, it is up to *us* to find out as much as we can about natural dog behaviour so that we can understand *why* our dog acts in certain ways. We will then be in a better position to modify our own behaviour and perhaps our surroundings, so that our dog finds it easier to live with *us*! After all, our dog probably thinks we are a problem when we don't take it for a walk, forget to feed it or leave it alone outside.

All breeds from the tiny Chihuahua to the enormous Great Dane have wolf ancestry, but the lifestyle of dogs and wolves is very different. Dogs don't have to hunt for food, water or a mate, and usually have very comfortable sleeping quarters, whereas the wolf has to fend for itself.

It may help us to understand our dogs if we know a little bit about how they evolved. It is believed that the first mammals appeared on earth about 150 million years ago but that they didn't make much impact until after the age of the dinosaurs 100 million years later. Unlike reptiles who eat infrequently, the mammals had a constant need for food. Many of them had to be hunters.

These early hunters were small creatures similar to weasels or civets. During the next 35 million years they adapted to changing environmental conditions and by about 15 million years ago one type of mammal called Tomarctus had taken on a distinct dog-like appearance. It too changed, so that approximately 3 million years ago our present day wolf emerged.

It was not until some 10,000 years ago that humans in different parts of the world began to domesticate the wolf, probably to help them to hunt, to keep them warm at night and to provide protection. In this relatively short pinprick of evolutionary time *we* have modified the wolf into the many varieties of breeds of dog we see today. No other domestic animal has been altered so dramatically into as many shapes and sizes, usually to the detriment of the natural dog! All to please our dubious aesthetic desires and to help us with questionable sporting pursuits! Many of the breeds of dogs which we have genetically manipulated would not be capable of surviving in the wild today.

However, these anatomical changes only continue because of human interference in the evolutionary process! If we were to put a male and female of every breed in a vast area capable of sustaining life, without human intervention we would quickly see some breeds die out and others modify to a more natural state. Probably the result would be a dog of medium size with pricked ears, strong limbs, deep chest, hanging tail and a fairly smooth coat, in other words a wolf or dingo-like dog. And this 'new' dog would have an extraordinary ability to survive. Why? Because today's dog has inherited most of the wolf's natural traits and behaviours, which have allowed it to survive for millions of years while other species have died out.

Humans have not changed the dog's way of behaving to any significant degree compared with the changes we have made to its physical structure. We have not added any behaviours like a dog talking or waving its paws, like hands. We have only modified the quality of its existing behaviours, often in a harmful way. Indeed, it is difficult to think of any improvement we have made to an existing behaviour which would be of benefit to the *dog*. We hope that we will never see changes to wolf behaviour, because their social structure and way of life is in many ways more peaceable and supportive than our own.

The aim of this book is to help you to keep your dog happy, healthy and socially acceptable so that you can gain as much as possible from your relationship.

It is important to be familiar with the laws and obligations associated with responsible dog ownership. Legal aspects are covered in Appendix A. Local government rules and regulations vary in each municipality and information can be sought from your local council.

You do not necessarily have to have a problem dog! Dog problems can be prevented if you understand what motivates dogs and how they learn. Existing problems can be cured if you are able to recognise what caused them in the first place and then know how to modify them in a simple efficient way without using any force.

Once you have read this book you will be able to develop ideas of your own on how to deal with dog problems which we haven't discussed, because problems certainly vary according to your own set of circumstances.

We acknowledge that there are a few dogs whose behaviour is almost impossible to change because they have developed long standing entrenched habits. Natural behaviours such as chasing are particularly hard to cure; however they **can** be controlled.

A small percentage of dogs are very aggressive and require the skills of an experienced professional dog trainer who may enlist the help of an understanding veterinarian. A combined approach is sometimes necessary.

An even smaller number develop physical conditions such as a brain tumour which can make their behaviour dangerously unpredictable. **Don't take any risks with these two types of dogs, particularly when children are around.** The majority of these dogs can be helped, but in some cases all the treatment in the world is to no avail.

The next chapter on how to avoid problems by bringing up the perfect dog, illustrates what we consider to be the ideal relationship between you and your dog.

While we've been working on this book we have been constantly questioning each other and challenging our own established beliefs about why dogs behave in the way they do. Every sentence has come under scrutiny. We have discussed, argued and dreamt about dogs! We would like you to go through a similar process as you read this book.

We hope that the following chapters on the development, senses and inherited behaviours of the wolf and dog will open the doors to a new and enlightened understanding of your own dog.

THE DOG'S ANCESTOR — THE WOLF

CHIHUAHUA — DIMINUTIVE SIZE

BRITISH BULLDOG — ALTERED STRUCTURE

AFGHAN HOUND — MODIFIED COAT LENGTH

BICHON FRISE — MODIFIED COAT TEXTURE

CHAPTER 2 PREVENTIVE MEDICINE
OR HOW TO BRING UP THE PERFECT DOG

They say that one man's meat is another man's poison! And so it is with the perfect dog. What one person thinks is perfection, another person may view as unacceptable! We want to show you how to bring up *your* perfect dog.

Inherent in our advice is an over-riding concern for the dog's quality of life. We are totally opposed to keeping dogs as commodities, for example leaving them isolated in the backyard to act as a guard. You and your dog should enjoy an excellent relationship if you follow the general principles below. Minor rules such as whether your dog is allowed on the bed are very much up to you as an individual. Some of the advice in this chapter is discussed again when we deal with the various behavioural problems.

1. Choose your breed carefully

Research the characteristics of various breeds carefully. Visit dog shows, talk to breeders and exhibitors, borrow books from the library and talk to your friends who have dogs. Realise that some people look at their favourite breed through biased eyes while others are more realistic! The temperament of the breed is more important than its looks. Frankly, some breeds are easier to live with than others. It is not within the scope of this book to discuss the features of breeds in any detail. However, a table in Appendix B lists our experience in regard to the trainability of various dogs. There is nothing against cross or mixed breeds except that you cannot be sure what behavioural characteristics they will inherit. When choosing a breed, look at its size, length of hair, the amount of exercise it requires, the cost of purchase and upkeep — but consider its temperament and trainability first. Make your choice, taking all these factors into consideration.

2. Get your dog at the best age

At what age should you acquire a dog? This is possibly *the* most important question and there is no flexibility about the answer! You should bring a puppy home between seven and eight weeks of age and *certainly* no older than nine. This will ensure that you have at least a few weeks of the critical socialisation period in which to expose your dog to as many experiences as possible. This is discussed more fully under point 6 on socialisation.

Getting an older dog can pose numerous problems because it will have established habits, some of which you may like, some of which you may not. Unfortunately, most of the older dogs who are looking for new homes are from various dog welfare organisations and most of them were put there because their owners could no longer cope with their behaviour. Some may even have been attack-trained (Problem 25). This is not the dog's fault but nor is it in your best interests to take on a dog with problems however well intentioned your motives. Organising a lobby group to persuade the government to restrict the breeding of dogs may be a more effective way of cutting down on the thousands of dogs who end up on death row each year.

3. *Acquire your dog from a reliable source*

Having chosen the type of dog you want, you should contact various breeders, either through personal recommendations, your local breed club or by answering advertisements in various canine magazines. It is best to contact the breeders first to assess their attitude and helpfulness and to find out whether they will have puppies available within a reasonable period. Have a list of questions ready to ask and expect to be interrogated in return! Responsible breeders want to make sure that *you* are a suitable owner for one of their puppies.

The next step is to visit the breeders who sounded helpful and responsible and look for, and ask about, the following:

1. Are the premises clean?
2. Can you meet the sire and dam of the potential puppies? Are they friendly and outgoing?
3. Have the parents been checked for genetic defects and, if so, does the breeder have evidence to show that they are relatively free of them?
4. Are the puppies raised in the house or in kennels?
5. Will they have regular individual contact and handling from different people?
6. Will the pups be wormed regularly?
7. At what age will they be immunised?
8. Will you be permitted to take a puppy home at seven to eight weeks of age?

Once you have selected the breeder you like best, then you may have to put your name on a waiting list for a pup.

4. *Choose your puppy carefully*

The litter has been born and you are now in a position to reap the benefits of your homework. Try to have as much contact with the puppies as practicable, starting when they are about three weeks old. Look for the 'middle of the road' pup who is neither too pushy nor always the last to explore.

Consider whether you want a male or female. Females are usually more placid and easy to live with, while a male may suit a more active type of person.

Males have a tendency to wander further afield as they mature and they sometimes show aggression to other entire male dogs. Remember this is a natural trait, see Chapter 5: Agonistic behaviour. Bitches can cause a problem for the keen gardener as their urine burns the lawn and, of course, females will either have to be spayed or kept away from male dogs when they are in season. When it comes to the final decision, you and your puppy will probably choose each other!

5. *Prepare for your puppy's homecoming*

You will require some basic equipment — two dishes, a brush and comb, a collar with identification tag, a long light lead, some sort of bed and some food. Find out what the breeder is using to feed the pups and make sure you have something similar. Change the diet gradually if you wish. A playpen will help you with your house training (Problem 7A).

Provide plenty of things which the puppy can be allowed to chew on and toys for it to play with. They often love pieces of rawhide and squeaky toys.

Your fences and gates must be secure and, if you go out to work, you should arrange to have at least two weeks' holiday if at all possible so that you can settle the puppy in. It is most important that you have time to establish your relationship with your puppy and to start socialising and training it. Of course you can enlist the help of friends or family instead, but then you will miss much of the fun and pleasure of those vital early weeks.

Make sure that the breeder has your puppy immunised and checked by a veterinarian at least ten days prior to the date you intend to take it home.

6. *Socialise your puppy*

SOCIALISATION KINTALA STYLE

What exactly is socialisation? It can be described as 'learning to take part in friendly interchange' or 'making a person or animal suited to fit into society'. Two very important attributes.

You will find out in Chapter 3 that the critical socialisation period for dogs is between the third and twelfth week after birth. It is terribly important that you use this knowledge to shape your puppy's behaviour and attitudes whilst it is in this particular phase of development. It is not possible to make up for lost time later in the pup's life.

Try to enrol in a puppy training course where your pup can mix and play with other dogs and their handlers, and where you can be taught basic control exercises. At the Kintala Club which David founded they have been running this type of course since 1976. Clients are given four lessons at weekly intervals by their own individual instructor. The pups are taught to come when called, to sit, stand and lie down on signal, to stay in those three positions for a short time, to walk beside the handler off lead and to do a basic retrieve. Before or after their training session, numerous puppies meet and play together for fifteen to thirty minutes.

The pups must be a minimum of eight weeks and a maximum of sixteen weeks old at the start of the course. Sometimes they are separated into two groups

PUPPY PLAY

so that the shyer or smaller ones do not become stressed. The pup's body language is watched carefully so that someone can intervene if necessary. A traumatic socialisation experience at this age can have a lasting detrimental effect, so care must be taken. Sometimes a nervous puppy which has had little contact with other dogs has to look on from the sidelines the first time it comes to 'school'. The handler is asked to sit on a bench to create a 'safe' area for the pup behind his or her legs. Usually this type of puppy ventures out and becomes as bold as the rest by lesson two. Occasionally it takes a bit longer.

Unfortunately it may be difficult to find a club which socialises dogs as young as eight weeks, in which case you will have to make your own arrangements. Try to meet up with other people who have healthy immunised puppies of a similar age and size. If this is impossible then go to visit friends who have quiet older dogs. Somehow you must make sure that your pup has regular contact with its own species.

Your pup should be handled by men, women and children of all ages. Give them some guidelines about how you would like your pup to behave so that they do not promote bad habits like jumping up (Problem 3).

Go out for short car trips which end with a romp in different parks so that the car is associated with pleasure and the pup experiences different environments. Take the pup to meet your neighbours, the postman, to see cars, a bus, a train, different animals, a river, the beach. In fact expose it to as many positive experiences as you possibly can. Later on you will have a dog that can cope with new experiences without becoming fearful or excited. In short, you will have a well socialised dog!

FRIENDLY CONTACT

7. Keep your puppy healthy

Unfortunately from our point of view, veterinary students are taught that they should advise their clients to keep puppies isolated in their house and garden until sixteen weeks of age when they have completed their immunisation regime. This may appear to be excellent advice in relation to the dog's physical health but we would be so bold as to say that it has actually been the death warrant for many thousands of animals. Why do we say this? There is fairly conclusive evidence that most of the dogs who end up in shelters are there because they have developed behavioural problems. Our experience tells us that these problems most frequently occur as a result of lack of socialisation during the critical socialisation period described in the last section.

Compare the many thousands of dogs who have to be put to death in shelters with the few who die of infectious diseases in puppyhood and you will get a more accurate picture of the relative risks! After all, if we said to a human mother 'don't take your child out because it might get a disease' she would rightly retort 'nonsense'. We recognise the need for our children to socialise. Why don't we recognise the dog's need?

The obvious solution is to **immunise** and **socialise** concurrently. Your puppy should be checked by your veterinarian soon after acquisition. You should discuss the possible need for additional immunisation over and above the usual regime of six, twelve and sixteen weeks to give your puppy maximum protection. A new vaccination regime currently being promoted in Australia is complete by twelve weeks of age. At the time of writing the results were inconclusive.

8. Start training your puppy as soon as you bring it home

Your puppy will learn rapidly whether you consciously teach it or not. Training your dog to be socially acceptable, for example *not* to jump up (Problem 3), is just as important as teaching it to stand, sit and lie down, for instance. Be absolutely consistent with your house 'rules' and stick to them.

House training should begin before the puppy even enters the house (Problem 7A).

We recommend that you buy our first book *Dog Training: The Gentle Modern Method* which will show

EARLY TRAINING FOR BOTH

you how to train your dog without using any force. This is extremely important for any dog, but particularly for puppies who are not able to tolerate the force and punishment used in the traditional compulsive method of training. The book also shows you how to avoid common handling errors. It is very easy to shape the behaviour of young puppies so that bad habits never develop.

The most important lessons are teaching your dog to come when it is called (Exercise 1) and to walk beside you on a loose lead (Problem 4).

9. Gently groom and handle your puppy

Your veterinarian will be very pleased if you teach your dog to remain quiet while it is examined. You can do this as follows:

1. Wait until your pup is tired after exercise and really keen for food. Cut up some small pieces of meat.

2. Approach the pup quietly when it is sitting (Exercise 2).

3. Touch various parts of the pup's body, offering a piece of food at the same time, so that the pup associates staying still and being touched with something pleasant.

4. After a few touches, progress to a point where you can touch the pup and *then* feed it immediately afterwards. Repeat this about ten times and then stop for the day.

5. Repeat these short sessions until you can gently open your pup's mouth, clean its ears or pick it up whenever you want without your pup showing any resentment or avoidance.

6. Start to offer food *intermittently* after handling so that the pup cannot predict when it will be fed.

NOTE: Remember to take a few pieces of choice food with you when you visit the veterinarian so that he or she can give your dog a reward after it is examined.

Information on how to use food appropriately and effectively in order to teach your dog is contained in Chapter 7: How Dogs Learn.

Follow a similar procedure when grooming your puppy, always keeping the sessions short and enjoyable and making sure that you do not do anything which is painful.

10. House train your puppy early

see Problem 7A.

11. Create good eating habits

see Problem 6E.

12. Provide regular exercise and regular rest

Your program of socialisation should ensure that your pup gets plenty of exercise! Regular mental stimulation will have the added benefit of actually increasing the size of its brain.

Remember that, like all babies, your pup needs plenty of rest too. Provide it with a quiet area, like a tea chest laid on its side or the playpen, in which to sleep in peace. Tired babies are fractious babies and a fractious puppy can start biting.

13. Stop your puppy from getting into the habit of biting

see Problem 8.

14. Allow the pup to be part of your family

One of the worst things that you can do to a social creature like the dog is to isolate it. In Chapter 5 we describe how the dog's ancestor, the wolf, lives in a highly organised co-operative pack. Because we take a pup away from its normal canine litter, we have to allow it to live in *our* social group. This does not mean that the puppy should not be outside for part of the day; in fact it will be healthier and happier if it is.

However, it should spend as much time as possible with the family.

Once your pup is house trained you should consider giving it free access to part of the house when you are out, so that it can come and go at will. This will prevent the development of the many behavioural problems which are associated with **boredom** (Problem 1).

CHAPTER 3 GROWING UP AS A DOG (OR WOLF)

Two notable American psychologists, Professor John Scott and Professor John Fuller, with their assistants studied dog behaviour for twenty years. They found that dog development could be classified into five periods:

1. The neonatal or new born period — birth to 13 days (approximately)

This is a period of life when the pups are highly adapted to living and surviving in a den. They can neither see nor hear and their ability to move is extremely limited because their brain is underdeveloped. Their capacity to learn is virtually non existent. The period ends when the pups' eyes open approximately thirteen days after birth.

As far as we are aware wolf cubs have never been observed in the wild during the neonatal and transitional periods of development. However, there is no reason to suppose that their behaviour is any different from puppy behaviour.

2. The transitional period — 13 to 20 days

This period gets its name because it is a time of transition between a very dependent and more adult type of behaviour. At this time the development of the senses gives the pups an increasing ability to respond to their environment. The motor nerves which control movement conduct stimuli more quickly so pups can move more rapidly, and travel further afield. The first signs of learning appear at about fifteen days.

HEELERS IN THE TRANSITIONAL PERIOD

3. *The socialisation period – 3 to 12 weeks*

The development of social relationships is an essential part of this period. It has been defined as *the critical period for socialisation*, which means that what the pups learn at this time from contact with other dogs, humans and other animals will have a *dramatic* effect in later life. It is therefore most important that pups are handled by a wide variety of people and exposed to as many different environments and situations as possible without becoming stressed. This not only helps them to grow into adults with a sound temperament who can readily cope with change, but it has been shown that extra stimulation actually makes the brain develop more.

Pups learn extremely rapidly from seven to eight weeks onwards when their eyesight has developed to adult capacity and they are able to move around fairly efficiently. This is when most people acquire a puppy and it is the optimum time for training to start.

We have discussed the implications of the socialisation period more fully in the previous chapter.

DOBERMANN IN THE SOCIALISATION PERIOD

4. *The juvenile period – 12 weeks to puberty*

This period starts when wolf cubs make their first long excursion from the den and ends at sexual maturity. Wolves mature in size and become physically capable of hunting so that they are fairly independent of their parents towards the end of this time. Dogs, however, are discouraged from hunting and we provide them with food 'on a plate' so to speak. Humans make dogs dependent way past the time when they would be independent in the wild, so we see behaviour typical of the socialisation and juvenile periods going on into adult life.

The life of a dog really starts to diverge from its ancestor the wolf throughout the juvenile stage. This is not what nature intended; it is purely a result of domestication. However, we must always remember that dogs will quickly revert back to natural behaviours if they need to do so to survive and are given the opportunity.

We have noticed that pups learn new responses very quickly between eight to sixteen weeks of age. After sixteen weeks they have usually developed a few habits which slow down the formation of new behaviours, e.g. if a dog has learnt to jump up, it will take a little

DOBERMANN IN THE JUVENILE PERIOD

longer to teach it to sit than if it had not learnt to jump up in the first place. Physical problems such as the gangly limbs of adolescence may also slow down the teaching procedure, e.g. it can take a little longer to teach a five month old Great Dane to lie down than an eight week old Labrador.

5. *The adult period — puberty to death*

The adult period extends from the time of sexual maturity until death. Adult wolves display their complete behavioural repertoire with the exception of most of the care seeking behaviours. They are independent and have no need to seek care from others. This contrasts sharply with domestic dogs who are obliged to seek care from us for the whole of their lives.

DOBERMANN IN THE ADULT PERIOD

CHAPTER 4 THE SENSES
AND HOW THEY AFFECT YOUR DOG'S BEHAVIOUR

The five major senses of sight, hearing, smell, touch and taste are our means of finding out about our environment. They affect each and every way we behave. Sometimes we find it hard to understand why animals behave in certain ways and this is usually because we have little knowledge of the scope of their senses. This sometimes makes us credit them with an extra sense when in actual fact they are simply using one of their existing senses in a way which we find hard to understand. For example, sharks hone in on the body electricity of their prey and can smell blood in the water from over half a kilometre away. Goldfish can see infrared and ultraviolet which are invisible to our eyes. Dolphins produce high pitched bursts of ultrasound which enable them to build up an x-ray type image of their prey and surroundings from the reflections of sound that they receive. All animals develop senses which help them to survive.

Dogs, too, have sensory abilities which are very different to our own. If we want to understand why dog behavioural problems develop, then we must learn something about these senses. This will help us to 'see' things from the dog's point of view!

1. The sense of sight

Without good eyesight a dog would not survive for long in the wild. Like humans, its sense of sight is stimulated continually while it is awake. The anatomy and position of its eye, if compared with the human eye, gives a more limited binocular vision, poor colour reception and an inferior awareness of detail. Hardly qualities consistent with survival! However, these deficiencies are more than adequately compensated for by the set of the eyes which gives them an extraordinary ability to notice the slightest movement over a wide area. They are interested in other ground running animals rather than tree-dwelling creatures,

A SCENE THROUGH HUMAN EYES

THE SAME SCENE THROUGH DOGS' EYES

because it is easier for them to kill animals on the ground. Most dogs are not interested in birds in trees, aeroplanes, telegraph wires or other objects which they can't reach. However, they react immediately to movement at ground level.

A study undertaken at the University of California in 1990 concluded that dogs can see a similar range of colours to humans who suffer from red/green colour blindness (deuteranopia). Deuteranopes can distinguish only about twenty-seven hues compared with the thousands of hues which people with normal colour vision can see. Apparently dogs can see the colours at one end of the spectrum, like violet, indigo and blue, quite clearly. Bluey green appears as white to them, while all the other colours are seen as shades of yellow. It is therefore very difficult for dogs to see the difference between green, yellow, orange and red, but easy for them to differentiate between blue and orange or red.

It will probably help if you wear at least one dark colour or a dark/light combination when exercising or training your dog so that it can easily see you moving against the background. Try it!

HOW THE DOG'S SIGHT MAY LEAD TO PROBLEMS IN A DOMESTIC ENVIRONMENT

1. Dogs are easily triggered into chasing fast moving objects especially at ground level. Cars, motorbikes, joggers, cats and sheep unfortunately come into this category! (Problem 13)
2. Dogs may try to escape from the confinement of a garden if they are stimulated by the sight of other dogs or people moving about on the other side of the fence. This happens more often when dogs are left isolated for most of the day. If the dog cannot escape it may run up and down the fence line, often barking at the same time, which may bring complaints from the neighbours. (Problem 18)
3. We have noticed that some dogs attack 'fluffy' dogs such as Samoyeds. We believe that this may happen because they are not able to read its body language correctly (Chapter 6). They may think that the fluffy dog is raising its hackles and respond as they feel the situation demands! (Problem 12B)
4. Garden fences often cause a dog to regard the house and garden as an artificial 'territory', in the same way as a wolf defends its den area. They often rush at the fence when they see someone go past, which may give passing pedestrians a terrible fright and result in injury if the dog gets out and drives them off with a nip. This is *natural* wolf behaviour! If the fence had never been there the dog would be much more likely to go up to the passer-by to investigate, without showing any aggression. (Problem 25)
5. Some dogs find it very difficult to see because they have so much facial hair which falls in front of their eyes. It should be kept short or pinned back to allow normal vision.

THE IMPORTANCE OF SIGHT WHEN MODIFYING BEHAVIOUR

1. Hand signals made at waist level or lower will attract more attention than those made above the head.
2. Moving hand signals will elicit more interest and action in the dog.
3. Alterations to hand signals, however slight, will tend to produce different responses in the dog.
4. Some inexperienced dogs find it difficult to locate food in the hand when they are first offered it. Sometimes they bite at fingers rather than what is in them! This can be remedied by presenting a clenched hand to the dog's mouth and then opening the fingers to reveal the food.

2. The sense of hearing

Hearing is measured in cycles per second (c.p.s.) or hertz. The human range is from a base tone of 20 c.p.s. to a high-pitched sound of approximately 20,000 c.p.s. Any sound over 20,000 c.p.s. is referred to as ultrasonic. Dogs can hear noises ranging from 20 c.p.s. to an amazing level of at least 35,000 c.p.s. Again this helps the dogs' survival, for many small animals such as rodents emit ultrasonic sounds and the dog can therefore use its hearing to find a meal!

Dogs learn to locate the source of a sound with great accuracy, using their large mobile ear flaps. Experiments have shown that they are able to pinpoint a sound within five degrees when it is placed anywhere in a circle of 360 degrees. It is interesting to discover how this skill develops by watching puppies at play, and then observing adult dogs. Puppies often look around them in some bewilderment when you call them. It takes them some time to locate you, particularly if you are standing still. The experienced adult dog does not have this problem unless its hearing has deteriorated with age or disease.

LOCATING SOUND

HOW THE DOG'S HEARING MAY LEAD TO PROBLEMS IN A DOMESTIC ENVIRONMENT

1. Dogs often react to ultrasonic sounds which are too high for us to hear! They may become excited and start running around or barking. Humans often react by saying 'Be quiet, there's nothing there!' (Problem 18)
2. Elderly animals sometimes become deaf which can make it appear as if they are ignoring your voice signals. If you think your dog is becoming deaf, increase your use of hand signals so, if it becomes completely deaf, you will still be able to communicate.
3. Dogs will quickly react to noises which signify enjoyment such as the sound of the family car engine, the tinkle of a lead taken off a hook, the sounds of food being prepared, or their owner's footsteps. This can lead to overly excitable behaviour. (Problem 11)
4. They are triggered to howl by highly pitched noises such as sirens and some music.

THE IMPORTANCE OF HEARING WHEN MODIFYING BEHAVIOUR

Dogs quickly react to high, sharp, sounds such as a gate latch, a key in a lock, or the sound of scissors cutting up slivers of meat. This suggests that dogs will be interested in similar voice signals and will be more likely to respond to them.

1. Dogs will always react to a hissing sound made through the teeth. Saying 'sit' or 'stand' in a similar way will elicit extreme interest.

2. It is always better to use high-pitched voice signals rather than low, commanding ones.

3. When calling a young puppy from a distance, it is better to move away from it while you say 'come', so that your movement will help the puppy to find the source of the sound.

3. *The sense of smell*

The incredible capacity of the dog's sense of smell has been proved by numerous scientific and practical tests. Dogs have been able to find people buried under many feet of snow. They can be trained to detect gas leaks underground, to sniff out drugs, and even to discover when a cow is in season.

Dogs' noses are very moist when they are scenting. Odour molecules dissolve into this thin mucus and the smell can then be carried by the nerve receptors to the brain.

Some authorities have suggested that the scent perception of dogs is 10 million times better than our own!

Why then do so many dogs who stray become lost, and unable to find their way home?

Wolves provide the answer. In their vast area of almost virgin territory, a wolf is not exposed to human smells, but simply to the trails of other animals. Even a wolf would get lost in suburbia. His sense of smell was not developed to cope with the numerous odours created by human beings and their urban lifestyle.

Nevertheless, dogs, like wolves, will demonstrate their remarkable scenting abilities when it comes to finding food. Wandering dogs easily hone in on rubbish bins! Food left in an accessible place around the house or the garden will quickly disappear — and we know where! Take a dog for a walk in the bush and it will invariably find some dead animal.

The dog's sense of smell can be affected by a

SCENTING

number of illnesses such as distemper, hepatitis, diabetes, hypothyroidism and tumours, or by irritation, infection or obstruction of the nose, and ageing.

Apparently the sense of smell of some bitches is less efficient before and during heat. We wonder if this is because she is more readily distracted at this time.

HOW THE DOG'S SENSE OF SMELL MAY LEAD TO PROBLEMS IN A DOMESTIC ENVIRONMENT

1. Dogs are often attracted to smells which we find abhorrent. Our Golden Retriever loves to roll in fresh horse manure and other nasty odours!

2. The smell of food from the kitchen bench may be a great temptation to some dogs. 'Stealing' may result! (Problem 6A)

3. Rubbish bins are a frequent drawcard for both domestic and feral dogs. Eating rubbish can be extremely dangerous due to the possibility of injury, poisoning or eating sharp bones which can puncture the intestine. In addition, the contents of bins strewn over the street is unsightly and a potential health and environmental hazard. (Problem 6B)

4. Dogs find some dangerous substances such as snail and rat bait very attractive and can easily be poisoned if these are placed where they can reach them.

The wolf and dog are both predisposed to think about food continually and they use their sense of smell to find it. This strong instinct can be utilised to our advantage when modifying undesirable behaviour in dogs.

4. *The sense of touch*

Human beings pat dogs basically for three reasons. Firstly, for the pleasure that stroking a warm fur coat can provide, secondly to pacify the dog, and thirdly to influence its behaviour. There is no denying the enormous satisfaction that dog lovers get from petting their dogs, but just what effect does our touch have on them?

Ever since human beings started walking on their hind legs, they have used their upper limbs to perform numbers of highly intricate and delicate movements. This ability has made them the most complex and destructive animals on earth. Dogs, like their ancestors, have never developed in this way and they use their upper or forelimbs just for basic survival techniques such as running after prey or finding a mate. They do not, for example, point or beckon with their legs, or scratch or caress one another with their paws. Dogs do not congratulate each other by patting each other on the back or shaking paws! The most elaborate responses are those between the mother and her young. Otherwise dogs only use their sense of touch when mouthing in greeting or play, sniffing, bumping one another, or engaging in sexual activity.

Because a dog's body is encased in a permanent cover of hair it presumably makes it less sensitive to pressure or temperature changes.

After years of observing dog behaviour we believe that dogs suffer from pain as we do, and also feel some pleasure in our physical contact with them. However, wolves have never used touch like human beings to show care, attention, and approval to each other and this self-reliant behaviour has been passed on to domestic dogs. All this may explain why dogs can take many knocks and bumps in their stride, and why they wag their tail when patted, but dismiss us quickly for another more meaningful stimulus like food (Chapter 7).

HOW THE DOG'S SENSE OF TOUCH MAY LEAD TO PROBLEMS IN A DOMESTIC ENVIRONMENT

1. Many training books advise dog owners to touch their dogs in an aversive way by hitting them with a rolled up newspaper, kneeing them in the chest, punishing them with a correction chain, or pulling their ears in an effort to stop unwanted behaviour. This leads to fear, resentment and avoidance behaviour on the part of the dog. (Problem 10A)
2. Fear is probably the most common reason for one dog attacking another; it attacks because it cannot find any other way of getting rid of the problem. (Problem 10B)
3. Avoidance behaviour creates difficulties in the show ring when a dog will not allow itself to be examined or bites the judge.
4. When dogs get wet, they naturally try to dry themselves. In the absence of grass, sand or earth they will use carpets, walls, soft furnishings or human legs!
5. Dogs scratch themselves when they feel itchy, especially during moulting or when they have fleas or an allergy, leaving a trail of hair wherever they go.
6. Dogs frequently lick at human skin, partly because it probably smells and tastes good and partly to stimulate care and attention from us, Chapter 5: Care seeking behaviour. There is a slight risk of transmitting disease when dogs lick children's faces.
7. Breeds with loose lips who salivate excessively such as Bloodhounds, Newfoundlands and Saint Bernards inadvertently rub saliva on our clothes and furnishings.

THE IMPORTANCE OF TOUCH WHEN MODIFYING BEHAVIOUR

1. Never use touch as a punishment because of the undesirable consequence mentioned on the previous page. This is explained more fully in Chapter 7.
2. Touching is extremely distracting to most animals because it may spell danger. If you push a puppy on its bottom to encourage it to sit down, it will tend to twirl around to investigate what is happening. Touch stimulus should be avoided when modifying behaviour except when a nervous dog is being taught to enjoy being handled.
3. Dog handlers often attach a great deal of importance to touch as a means of affecting their dog's behaviour. We cite a simple experiment on page 47 which compares the use of patting with the use of food as a means of rewarding or reinforcing responses. It is very clear to us that the use of touch for this purpose is an extremely inefficient method of teaching.

5. *The sense of taste*

A dog's sense of taste is not utilised until it has been stimulated by another sense, such as smell, hearing or sight. For example, a wolf hears a sound, looks up to investigate it, and sees a small animal running along the ground. He chases and captures the animal using his senses of sight, hearing, touch and smell and then eats his prey. His sense of taste is the last sense to be stimulated.

HOW THE DOG'S SENSE OF TASTE MAY LEAD TO PROBLEMS IN A DOMESTIC ENVIRONMENT

Dogs eat very rapidly. If something smells good, they usually swallow it quickly without stopping to savour the taste. Unfortunately this can lead to death by poisoning.

THE IMPORTANCE OF TASTE WHEN MODIFYING BEHAVIOUR

1. Taste alone cannot be used to modify behaviour.
2. Dogs, like humans, develop preferences for certain foods.
3. When offering food as a form of reward we should use the dog's favourite type. Most dogs prefer meat.

CHAPTER 5 INHERITED BEHAVIOUR IN THE DOG AND WOLF

What is behaviour?

It is not yet possible to enter into the mind of any creature and understand its every thought; heaven help the world if we could ever do this! However, we can observe the consequences of most 'thought' processes when they lead to behaviours. When an animal responds to a stimulus we call this response a behaviour.

At the beginning of this century some scientists who were studying the learning process in animals started to use a new method. They recorded every behaviour of the animal that they could observe. This gave them answers to the question 'Why do animals behave in a particular way?'

Behaviourists, as these people were called, grouped behaviours which were linked in some way into a number of *behavioural systems*, for example the acts of urination and defecation were classified under the eliminative system.

Professors John Scott and John Fuller, whose research we mentioned in Chapter 3, grouped the ninety behaviours which they had observed in dogs of different ages into nine behavioural systems:

1. Investigatory (exploring the environment)
2. Ingestive (eating and drinking)
3. Eliminative (urinating and defecating)
4. Care seeking (looking for care and attention)
5. Shelter seeking (sheltering from the environment)
6. Agonistic (degrees of boldness and timidity; competitive and hunting behaviours)
7. Group (doing things with other dogs)
8. Sexual (looking for and finding a mate)
9. Care giving (looking after the young and looking after yourself)

When they examined reports of wolf behaviour in the wild, particularly the descriptions of Murie, Young and Goldmann, and Schenkel, they found that all but nineteen of the behaviours displayed by North American wolves were also displayed by dogs. The nineteen missing behaviours were mostly related to hunting and catching prey, behaviours which we actively discourage in the dog for obvious reasons. No doubt these behaviours would be displayed by dogs who have to fend for themselves.

All this goes to show that, basically, you have a wolf in your living room! Although we have created a propensity in certain *breeds* to herd and retrieve for instance, these same dogs would quickly kill if the need arose. In other words they would revert back to their 'norm'.

Many of the so called problems which we encounter in dogs are a result of stresses caused by changes to their environment and social order which dogs have to cope with when living with a human family.

For example, can we expect a dog whose ancestors lived in a pack structure to be happy and quiet when it is left isolated in a backyard for long stretches of time? Of course it will try to entertain itself by 'being naughty', 'getting into mischief', 'barking all the time' and so on.

By studying the natural behaviour of the dog and the wolf, we will not only be able to understand our pet better, but we will be in a position to offer it a more natural and fulfilling lifestyle. Because of this, we will be able to minimise or eliminate many of the problems which **we** have generated.

An explanation of our colour coding system

The nine behavioural systems of the dog have been colour coded as follows:

1. Investigatory
2. Ingestive
3. Eliminative
4. Care Seeking
5. Shelter Seeking
6. Agonistic
7. Group
8. Sexual
9. Care giving

The following symbols are also used in this chapter and when we deal with problem behaviours in the second part of this book:

● a dot in any colour indicates that the problem is related to natural wolf or dog behaviour.

✚ a cross in any colour indicates that the problem is due to dog behaviour which we have modified by domestication.

The colour of the dot or cross shows which behavioural system the problem behaviour is classified under, e.g.

● = natural investigatory behaviour

✚ = modified eliminative behaviour

It is useful to know if a problem behaviour is natural or whether it has been caused by domestication. It is also important to know to which behavioural system it is related, as this will help us to find the best way of changing it. Some behaviours are very deep rooted while others are relatively easy to modify — it all depends how important they are to the natural dog.

Our colour coding cuts down on the need for detailed explanations when we mention the causes of problem behaviour later in this book. We have repeated it at the foot of each page in the problem section to save you having to turn back to this chapter too often.

1. Investigatory behaviour

Exploring the environment by using the senses of sight, hearing, smell, touch and taste

Investigatory behaviour is closely linked to many of the other systems, especially to agonistic, ingestive and group behaviour when hunting, and to sexual and eliminative behaviour when finding a mate.

Newly born puppies are incapable of investigating their world except in a very limited way by the use of touch and taste. It is not until the eyes and ears open at approximately the thirteenth and nineteenth days of life respectively, and the pup becomes physically more able to use its legs efficiently that exploration starts in earnest. From this moment on, both wolves and dogs use their senses to investigate during every waking moment. Even when half asleep they will open an eye, cock an ear or lift their heads to sniff the air. Such behaviour is essential to their survival.

Wolves are hunting animals and they must constantly be on the alert for a possible meal. They also explore over a wide area in order to find a mate and to find out whether other wolves are in the vicinity. Wolves use their eyes, ears and noses for hunting, utilising whichever sense is most appropriate for the occasion.

INVESTIGATORY BEHAVIOUR

Some breeds of dogs have been modified so that they use one of their senses predominantly, for example long-legged sight hounds, such as the Deerhound, will chase swift moving prey over large open areas where scenting is not very important, while scent hounds like the Bloodhound can track a scent without being able to see the prey animal running away. Obviously these attributes are useful if the dog owner wishes to utilise them, but sometimes they can cause problems too! Beagles who run with their noses close to the ground are readily stimulated to follow a scent trail. A movement some distance away will trigger a whippet into speedy pursuit. Either event can mean a long walk home for the owner!

Wolves and all breeds of dogs will investigate each other socially mainly by sniffing each other's faces and genitalia. Unfortunately many dogs cannot explore naturally because they are often restrained on a lead when taken for a walk, or confined to a backyard, and this leads to many, many problem behaviours which are related to pure boredom!

POTENTIAL PROBLEMS RELATED TO INVESTIGATORY BEHAVIOUR IN DOMESTIC DOGS

● Dogs bred for scenting may constantly sniff the ground and wander far afield following a scent. (Problem 5B)

● Dogs bred for hunting by sight may be highly stimulated by fast moving animals or birds.

+ Similarly they will tend to chase cars and motorbikes. (Problem 13B)

● Both dogs and bitches may investigate far afield in search of food or a mate. (Problem 26)

+ Dogs who are not allowed to investigate each other naturally may become aggressive when other dogs come close to them, especially if they are restricted by a lead or chain. (Problem 12A)

● Puppies frequently mouth and bite. (Problem 8)

+ Dogs frequently jump up on people or at doors in order to investigate them.

BOREDOM-RELATED BEHAVIOURS CAUSED BY A LACK OF OPPORTUNITY TO INVESTIGATE

A dog which is contained in a restricted area such as a backyard is stimulated by the same things day after day. It does not experience the excitement of exploring new surroundings. As a result it will react excessively to the few stimuli which do occur, for example:

1. Barking constantly at a neighbour's dog. (Problem 18)
2. Hanging on the washing. (Problem 16)
3. Digging an even bigger hole in the garden. (Problem 15)
4. Running up and down the fence line. (Problem 19)
5. Chewing up pot plants. (Problem 14)
6. Making repetitive movements like chasing its tail, pouncing or snapping at water. (Problem 17)

Summary: The investigatory behaviour of wolves and dogs is essentially the same, except that dogs often have a limited range and opportunity. Many breeds have been modified to investigate, using one sense predominantly.

2. Ingestive behaviour

Eating and drinking

The most obvious difference between the eating behaviour of dogs and wolves is that in most cases wolves will eat in a group, while dogs usually have their own dish. Wolves may share the entire carcass of a large animal, including meat, hair, bones, offal and the viscera containing predigested vegetable matter. They may consume enormous quantities, up to 8 kilos at a time, especially if it is a few days since their last meal. Wolves also eat smaller prey which they catch and kill independently.

Dogs are offered smaller amounts more frequently, usually once a day because this suits our schedule. We tend to feed them with smaller pieces of food than they would eat in the wild, including meat, soft tinned food, dry food and scraps. Although the diet we offer is usually nutritionally sound it does not exercise the dog's teeth, jaws and digestive system as nature intended.

Wolves may go for up to a week without eating and not suffer any harm. Our dogs could probably do the same if necessary. Missing a meal one day is of little significance to them, although most dogs look expectantly at their owners at feeding time out of habit.

Adult method of eating

Both wolves and dogs eat rapidly without chewing; in other words they 'wolf their food down'. The reason for this, of course, is survival. Most hunting animals must eat as much as they can in as short a time as possible. After all, there are many other predators on the look out for an easy meal!

Food is ingested by picking it up with the teeth, then releasing the food and quickly lowering the head to throw the food to the back of the mouth where it is swallowed rapidly. Saliva lubricates the food and helps it to be dispatched quickly. Eating is done in the standing position with the tail held low. Bones and large chunks of meat may be eaten lying down and sometimes the paws are used for holding.

Liquid is taken in by scooping fluid up with the tongue and frequently making quite a mess in the process!

Wolves and dogs carry heavy bones by holding them in the jaws with the head held high. They trot along, watching carefully for anyone who might take their prize from them. Surplus food, especially bones, may be buried around the wolves' den area to prevent other predators from taking it, and to keep it 'fresh'.

Dogs also exhibit this behaviour when they are full, much to the annoyance of some owners! A hole is dug with the paws, the food dropped in and then the nose is used to cover the food by pushing material on top of it and tamping it down. Dogs occasionally try to bury their food dishes in the same way, and this is a clear indication that they are being overfed!

It is normal for both wolves and dogs to eat grass and they seem to prefer the moist, broad bladed species. Grass probably acts as a form of roughage. From our observations dogs do not eat grass when they are unwell to make themselves vomit as is commonly supposed.

INGESTIVE BEHAVIOUR

Puppies and cubs' method of eating

Almost as soon as they are born puppies and cubs feed from their mothers by sucking milk. They pull back on the nipple frequently and, at the same time, knead their mother's abdomen with their paws. At about three weeks of age humans start to supplement the bitch's milk with other soft food.

Wolves prepare their own special puppy food by regurgitating warm, partly digested food, for the cubs. This behaviour is not confined to the mother. The father and older siblings also help to feed them. If the mother dies, other wolves may successfully rear the cubs.

Mother dogs sometimes regurgitate food for their young, but this is often discouraged by the owner. To our knowledge male dogs have not been seen to do this, but perhaps this is because they are usually not intimately involved with rearing their young.

When the pups are about three or four weeks old, the bitch begins to stand while nursing them and by five weeks she may begin to growl when they try to suck. This gradual weaning process finishes about seven to ten weeks after the birth when the bitch's milk dries up. Pups are capable of eating like adults when the permanent teeth erupt between four and six months of age.

POTENTIAL PROBLEMS RELATED TO INGESTIVE BEHAVIOUR IN DOMESTIC DOGS

● Dogs are opportunistic feeders and some breeds in particular will eat whenever the opportunity arises. This may include anything from raiding dustbins to eating the cat's food or stealing the roast dinner! (Problem 6)

● It is natural for dogs to dig holes to bury bones.

They really don't understand that they shouldn't dig up your newly planted seedlings in the process! (Problem 15)

● Dogs who are not familiar with one another may compete for food, just as a pack of wolves would chase a strange wolf from their kill, see Agonistic behaviour.

+ People who feed their dogs too frequently may cause picky eating habits. (Problem 6E)

+ Eating faeces. (Problem 7F)

Summary: Left to their own devices, the ingestive behaviour of wolves and dogs is almost identical. Humans have altered the amount and texture of the dog's food and its frequency of eating.

---

3. Eliminative behaviour

Urinating and defecating

A knowledge of the eliminative behaviour of dogs and wolves is a great help when it comes to house training, for one thing we learn is that pups or cubs rarely, if ever, soil their sleeping area. The implications of this will be discussed fully in Problem 7A.

Until pups or cubs are physically capable of leaving their den or bed area their mother licks their bellies to stimulate them to urinate and defecate. By licking up the deposits she keeps the area clean. Once they start to move around at two to three weeks old the pups start to eliminate outside the sleeping area. Females squat to urinate while male pups stand and urinate in a similar manner to a horse.

Around puberty males start to lift their legs and direct a small amount of urine on raised objects such as trees or rocks. This has the effect of leaving their odour at a height which is easier for other dogs to sniff

ELIMINATIVE BEHAVIOUR

and, just as importantly, the visual landmark attracts other dogs to investigate that spot. Females occasionally lift their legs, too, but they do so by lifting one hind leg under their body rather than in the standard male way of lifting one leg out laterally. It has been suggested that the different positions adopted for urination helps dogs identify the sex of another dog at a distance. Leg lifting in males does not seem to be affected by the male hormone testosterone, as males who have been castrated prior to puberty also lift their legs. Leg lifting is inhibited if no strange males come into another dog's area. In other words, males will not spray on top of their own mark; they wait until another dog has urinated on the same spot.

Marking behaviour does not have the territorial significance that most people imagine. Wolves only defend the small area around their den. It would be impossible for them to regularly patrol and defend the enormous perimeter of their hunting ground. Studies have shown that wolf packs remain in fixed and stable areas which may overlap for up to 2 kilometres. Wolves tend to increase marking when they come across fresh signs of a neighbouring pack which results in a concentration of smells along the borders of each area. Presumably this inhibits both packs from impinging on each other's area and limits the number of animals which are hunting in one place. Stopping to sniff fresh marks may also slow another pack down, making it less likely for the two packs to come in contact.

The domestic dog unconsciously goes through a similar marking ritual but the effect is not the same because it is not possible for the normal inhibitory function of marking, which keeps packs of wolves apart, to function in suburbia. There are simply too many dogs concentrated in a small area to make this possible.

Marking does not stop one dog from entering another dog's territory. We can therefore deduce that the main social reasons for marking behaviour are to bring a male in contact with a female in heat and to limit contact between wolf packs. It also helps lone wolves to form their own group.

Elimination is closely associated with sexual behaviour and is a most important social tool in the lives of wolves and dogs. Females who are in heat start to deposit small amounts of urine further afield than normal. Special scents in her urine called phernomes tell male dogs that she is almost ready for mating. It appears that males must come in close contact with her urine and secretions in order to find this out. All our observations indicate that her scent does not appear to be carried on the air for any distance. This has practical significance in managing a bitch in heat in suburbia which will be discussed under Problem

26. A mated pair will double mark which probably tells lone wolves that a mated pair already live in the area and that they should look for a territory elsewhere.

Wolves and dogs defecate in the same way. Both sexes squat down and males, in particular, may scratch the ground afterwards. This does not have the effect of covering the faeces but probably acts as an additional visual signal for other members of the species. It is thought that the smell of the faeces is different in each animal due to glands situated inside the anus and that this is a valuable form of identification. Sweat glands between the paws may also signal the characteristic odour of individual animals.

POTENTIAL PROBLEMS RELATED TO ELIMINATIVE BEHAVIOUR IN DOMESTIC DOGS

- Young puppies urinating in the house. (Problem 7A)
- Older dogs urinating in the house. (Problem 7B)
- Fear or excitement induces urination. (Problem 7C, D)
- Male dogs 'marking' in a strange house. (Problem 7E)
- Defecating in the house. (Problem 7A, B)
- Males tracking females in heat. (Problem 26)
- Increased agonistic behaviour due to limited

home territory which does not allow the inhibitory effect of marking behaviour to function.

Summary: The method and intent of elimination is the same in wolves and dogs. The sheer number of dogs in our society and their limited home territory results in many more strange animals coming into contact with one another. Marking behaviour would inhibit such contact in the wild.

---

4.   Care seeking behaviour

Looking for care and attention
Most of the attention or care seeking behaviour is shown between birth and four months of age, although play soliciting behaviour between older dogs and wolves could be construed as a form of seeking attention.

Newly born pups whine and yelp in distress when separated from the rest of the litter. They crawl slowly in a circle, mainly using their forelimbs while moving their head from side to side, until they contact something warm which they move towards. They also vocalise when cold or hungry, which produces appropriate care giving responses on the part of the bitch.

At three to four weeks when pups become more active and are able to leave the nest, they run to the mother in the case of dogs, or a family member in the case of wolves, and lick and paw at their face and

CARE SEEKING BEHAVIOUR

chest. This stimulates the older animals to regurgitate, or vomit, food for them.

Once wolves are physically able to join the hunt and fend for themselves, there is little need for them to seek care from others. However, they continue to seek attention in play activities and may also howl when they are separated from the rest of the pack during a hunt. Howling is mainly a method of communication used to bring the pack together, but it could also be interpreted as both group, and attention seeking, behaviour.

Older dogs are a rather different kettle of fish, probably because we keep them very dependent on us for all their basic needs. We can all think of a myriad of ways in which our dogs try to gain our attention:

1. Pawing at our hands or legs.
2. Barking or scratching to get into the house when left outside alone.
3. Pushing their noses under our hands to get us to stroke them.
4. Bringing their dishes to us is a clear effort to indicate 'I'm hungry' or 'I'm thirsty'.
5. Looking expectantly at the door when it's time to go out for a walk or to relieve themselves.
6. Dropping sticks or toys at our feet to stimulate us to throw them.

If we look at this list objectively, we can see that all these behaviours are the result of human conditioning rather than any fundamental difference in behaviour between wolves and dogs. If our dogs were permitted to become feral they would not *need* to rely on us. Logically, then, we must accept that any problems that arise out of their dependence on us are self-inflicted and that we must take responsibility for causing them! We will talk about solving these problems further on in this book.

POTENTIAL PROBLEMS RELATED TO CARE SEEKING BEHAVIOUR IN DOMESTIC DOGS

+ Overly dependent behaviour – excessive whining, pawing. (Problem 20)
+ Jumping up at people to gain attention. (Problem 3)
+ Constant barking when left alone. (Problem 18)
+ Scratching at windows and doors. (Problem 3)
+ Chewing objects during teething. (Problem 14)

Summary: Dogs have expanded their repertoire of attention and care seeking behaviours only because of their dependence on humans. We must therefore take responsibility for fulfilling their physical needs and their need for continuous social contact.

5. Shelter seeking behaviour

Sheltering from the environment

Shelter seeking behaviour is not well developed in wolves. Only when they are raising cubs do they create a special sheltered den area by enlarging holes made by other animals, or by using caves. The bitch scratches out a bit of ground to make it comfortable, but she does not make a nest as such. The cubs are very reliant on this sheltered area as they have very poor temperature control during the first one to two weeks of life and stay heaped together in the den to conserve heat.

Female dogs, on the other hand, are rarely allowed to choose where they want to give birth. They may shred paper or scratch the floor where they are going to whelp in an effort to make a little hollow for themselves. Puppies are usually born in a larger area than a wolf cubs' den and so it may be necessary for their owners to raise the air temperature with the use of heating pads or radiators. If one pup becomes separated from the rest, the bitch will quickly pick it up and return it to the rest of the litter.

Adult wolves do not actively look for shelter but they will circle around a few times on the same spot before lying down, and may lie curled up with their noses buried in their tails for extra heat conservation. The natural insulation of their thick coats is so good that they have been observed to lie stretched out on their sides in the snow. Their pelt is adapted to the particular climatic conditions where they live.

Dogs are usually provided with shelter, often of a luxurious kind! Humans have modified their coats by selective breeding and we see a tremendous variety, ranging from the hairless Chinese Crested to the double coated Spitz breeds and the long haired Afghan hound. This may have led dogs to adopt a greater variety of postures while resting, including lying frog-like on their bellies with their back legs out behind them or lying on their backs with legs spread-eagled! We can find no record of wolves being observed in these positions.

Shelter seeking behaviour also includes taking refuge from too much heat! Dogs will dig large holes in the dirt or may excavate under the house in an effort to find a cool shady spot. Some breeds, in particular, learn that lying in shallow water is absolute bliss on a hot day and many enjoy swimming. Presumably northern wolves would not choose to go into icy water primarily to keep cool, but they have been observed to go into water to catch fish.

SHELTER SEEKING BEHAVIOUR
A COOL SHADY SPOT

POTENTIAL PROBLEMS RELATED TO SHELTER SEEKING BEHAVIOUR IN DOMESTIC DOGS

● Dogs tend to dig large holes in the dirt to keep cool. (Problem 15)

✛ They often bark to get into the house when it is cold or wet. (Problem 18)

● They may circle around in flowerbeds before lying down on our favourite seedlings!

✛ Some dogs occasionally try to dig 'holes' in the carpet or cushions. (Problem 15)

Summary: Shelter seeking behaviour is not well developed in wolves; their natural coat protects them even in very harsh conditions. Humans have modified the coats of most breeds of dogs so that they are not necessarily suitable for the climate where the dog lives. Dogs are reliant on humans to clip and/or groom them, and to provide adequate protection from the elements.

6. Agonistic behaviour

Degrees of boldness and timidity; competitive and hunting behaviours

Wolves and dogs are both classed as carnivores, which means that they are both flesh-eating mammals. If an animal is a carnivore, it is a hunter. To be a hunter it must be bold and aggressive. Some carnivores are solitary animals, others like the wolf live in groups. Over the centuries the words 'wolf pack' have conjured up in people's minds an image of vicious and blood-thirsty animals that will kill anything in their path, including humans.

Fortunately, scientific research over the last fifty years has discredited these myths, leaving us with the knowledge that wolves live as a family, expressing care and friendliness to one another. Unhappily, this cannot be said of some breeds of dogs that have been bred specifically for increased aggression and are unable to live peaceably together!

The formation of a wolf group is largely dependent on a mating between a superior male and female. They may breed for a few years, producing up to six pups a year. Taking into consideration the high mortality rate because they live in a very harsh and unforgiving environment, a small family group will be gradually established. The differences in age, size, boldness and experience govern the interactions between the various members of the group so that each understands its place in the family structure. Just as a young human child accepts the fact that its parents are more knowledgeable, a wolf cub instinctively knows that older wolves are superior, whether they are older brother, sister or parent. An established hierarchy means there is little need to express dominance.

Parent wolves influence most of their cubs' behaviour with tolerance and without force, an attribute often missing in human relationships! For example, wolf parents do not grab their pups by the scruff of the neck and give them a shaking. This is a common misconception frequently cited by people who try to justify the use of punishment when training dogs. Scientific observations of wolves in the wild indicate that they use body language in an almost deliberate attempt to avoid confrontation, see Chapter 6. This obviously helps the wolves to survive as a species. It has been suggested by people who have observed them in the wild that the human race could learn a great deal from this friendly family animal. Wolves prefer to keep away from the unpredictable and aggressive human race. Throughout North America there has never been a wolf attack on a human being except when the wolf has been mad with rabies. There is an amusing comment supposedly said by an old trapper: 'Anyone who says they have been ate by a wolf is a liar!'

Socialisation within a wolf group continues from the time of birth to the time of death. Domestic dog puppies only have a brief period in their lives from birth to eight weeks of age when much socialisation is permitted, and this is usually limited to their mother, litter mates and breeders. Rarely does the father have the opportunity to mix with his pups, nor do young adults from previous litters. This behaviour which has been natural for millions of years is now impractical in our society.

We have observed that a puppy which is taken away from its litter mates at approximately six weeks of age will often show a strong affinity to its human owners but less tolerance towards other dogs. Conversely, a puppy that has stayed with its litter mates until sixteen weeks of age often displays an independent attitude towards humans but has an ability to assimilate with other dogs. Most importantly a puppy which has not been exposed to a variety of different environments up to the sixteenth week of age will find it more difficult to accept and adjust to change. We have discussed the implications of these last three sentences in Chapter 2.

Wolf and dog puppies develop their boldness by degrees. It is not possible to pick up a puppy of less than three weeks of age and predict that it is going to be the boldest, or the most timid, in the litter. At this age their senses are not yet fully developed and they are not physically capable of testing each other's strengths and weaknesses. However, the heavier puppies in the litter unconsciously exert some pressure on the rest, especially at suckling time.

As the senses become more developed and their physical ability to explore increases, the myriad of interactions between the puppies starts to form the basic character or temperament of each animal. Puppies haphazardly bump into one another, which often develops into awkward mouthing mostly around the face and neck. By five weeks of age these actions are more deliberate. It is a period of assertiveness. Puppies who are successful in play fighting will become bolder, showing an increased tendency towards aggression. Constant losers will lose the desire to interact and will display avoidance behaviour.

Those that have a fair share of wins and losses will develop a more balanced temperament and often make better pets.

At approximately twelve weeks of age wolf cubs take their first long excursion from the den area in preparation for joining in hunting activities. Competition for regurgitated food is now in earnest. Survival depends on agility, speed and, to some extent, aggression. Wolf cubs are fed irregularly and this creates an eagerness for food which increases their determination to learn to hunt successfully. It takes a great deal of courage, persistence and boldness to come into conflict with such large animals as caribou and moose. Their flashing hooves and enormous antlers can inflict mortal wounds. Physical examination of dead wolves invariably shows numerous scars, most of which are attributed to these large herding animals. Wolves must recuperate quickly after an injury in order to resume their search for food. Dogs express a similar desire to get on with life after injury or surgery, in contrast with humans who sometimes seem to enjoy the sickness role!

Hunting animals such as wolves and feral dogs are unable to determine where or when their next meal will be. It would be a sorry situation for prey animals if predators could locate and catch a meal at will. If wolves were successful every time they hunted caribou, we would see a considerable decline of these grazing animals and a population explosion of wolves! It is estimated that 90 percent of wolf attacks on herding animals are unsuccessful. The speed of the caribou always gives it the winning edge in a chase. Wolves usually chase an old, sick, injured or smaller animal which runs more slowly than the rest of the herd and this has a natural culling effect.

It may be a week or even longer before a group of wolves can make a kill. Then it is feasting time! Their ingestive system is geared for a feast or famine existence. However, because feasting is not a predictable event wolves will seize the opportunity to eat at any time and will hunt prey such as rodents individually. In other words, wolves are predisposed to think about food for much of their waking life. This attitude towards food is also observed in most breeds of domestic dogs. A dog which is taken for a walk after its evening meal will still gobble up odd bits of food found along the way. If a rabbit crosses its path it will still give chase. The mere movement of the rabbit is enough to trigger this hunting behaviour – to catch, to kill, to eat, to survive.

Wolves from different groups sometimes cross each other's path. When they meet face to face their reactions are almost identical to those of dogs. Superior wolves and dogs convey their intentions by enlarging their physical appearance, holding their heads high and ears erect, flicking a stiff tail, raising their hair and stiffening their legs to look imposing. Inferior wolves do just the opposite.

After examination of each other's noses and genitalia the usual sequence of events is for both animals to break contact. If the animals concerned are males, they may move to the nearest object and urinate on it. They sometimes repeat this procedure and afterwards go their separate ways. Aggression is unlikely when this natural behaviour can occur.

The effective use of body language (Chapter 6) practically always defuses potential confrontations and preserves social harmony within the group. Sometimes, however, the system fails and acts of aggression do occur. The most serious events take place during the pre-mating period. Superior wolf bitches become very snappy and try to stop other bitches in the pack from mating. Superior males discourage attempts by lesser males to mate. Some lower ranking individuals see themselves as equal to those further up the hierarchy and serious confrontations can result which may even change the social order of the group.

Fighting amongst wolves is very similar to their attacks on prey. There is a lot of darting in and out, and snapping at each other's flanks and legs. When wolves attack a caribou they slash at its legs in order to slow it down, then one wolf may make a frontal attack and grab it by the nose.

Wolves have been known to gang up on one individual in their pack in what appears to be an effort to ostracise it from the main group. This may be a culling action designed to eliminate a member which shows inadequacies in its behaviour.

A lone wolf that tries to join another group is likely to be sent packing with a few cuts and bruises for good measure. It is rare for these wolves to be accepted into an established group and they are forced to live alone

AGONISTIC BEHAVIOUR

or join up with another lone wolf and so establish their own family group.

Restrictions imposed by fences, leads, owners and local authorities give suburban dogs little opportunity to hunt. Nearly all breeds of dog would hunt if given the chance. Man has modified this basic drive in some breeds for his own dubious reasons. Retrievers are allowed to retain one natural aspect of the hunt, that is, the desire to seek and find. What follows is bizarre. They gently pick up the dead or injured animal and bring it to the shooter. Similarly Setters and Pointers hunt, but their final act is even stranger. They just stand and point their body in the direction of hidden prey. Herding dogs have had the final act of hunting modified so that they do not attack, injure or kill.

None of these modified behaviours would be retained if these dogs were returned to the wild. Their need to survive would quickly establish normal, natural responses.

Dogs rarely have the opportunity to form stable packs and their home area is extremely limited in size because of our use of fences. The average large garden is probably very similar in size to the area around a wolf's den and dogs will react accordingly by defending it. It must be pointed out that these aggressive responses are intensified by the abnormal barrier of fences which do not allow normal canine communication to take place. It is not feasible to remove our fences in a suburban environment but, if we could, we would inevitably see a lessening of aggression in dogs provided that there were not too many animals interacting within a very small area.

POTENTIAL PROBLEMS RELATED TO AGONISTIC BEHAVIOUR IN DOMESTIC DOGS

- Male dogs attacking other male dogs. (Problem 12A)
+ Dogs biting adults or children. (Problem 6D and 12E)
- Killing domestic stock such as chickens or sheep. (Problem 13A)
- Dogs sometimes compete for food. (Problem 6C, D)
+ 'Defending' territory such as the house, garden or car. (Problem 25)
+ Rushing at the fence surrounding the house and/or rushing out at passers by.
+ Chasing fast moving objects such as cars and motorbikes. (Problem 13B)
- Fear related submissive behaviour. (Problem 10)

+ Fear of men, women, people wearing hats, etc. (Problem 10A)
+ Phobias, e.g. extreme fear of thunderstorms, fireworks, etc. (Problem 10C, D)

Summary: Wolves and dogs naturally control their aggression towards each other by the effective use of body language. Acts of aggression occur more frequently during the mating period in wolves. Unnatural restraint increases the likelihood of aggression in dogs. Some breeds have been selectively bred for increased aggression. For obvious reasons dogs rarely have an opportunity to hunt.

7. Group behaviour

Doing things with other dogs

Group behaviour is fundamental to the survival of wolves. Animals who live in a pack are in a much better position to hunt and kill large prey successfully and to defend the immediate den area and their cubs. Wolves usually stay in close proximity to one another, although they sometimes separate to hunt for game.

It is interesting to notice how our dog's natural instinct to stay in a group is demonstrated in our daily lives. Our own two dogs walk, run and do things in the garden with us, they flop down on the floor close to us when we sit in the lounge room, and sleep on the bed at night! They even move from room to room as we cook, type, clean or watch TV; in other words we have become their pack. Wolves display the same characteristics with one another.

Group behaviour starts to develop soon after puppies are able to crawl around and, by the time they are five weeks old, they will rush together to investigate anything new.

We have found that puppies have a strong inclination to follow their 'human' family until they are about twelve weeks old when they start to explore more independently. This corresponds with the time when wolf cubs would start moving further away from the den to explore. We use this to our advantage by training young puppies to come when called before they reach twelve weeks, so capitalising on their natural tendency to want to stay close to us!

GROUP BEHAVIOUR

POTENTIAL PROBLEMS RELATED TO GROUP BEHAVIOUR
IN DOMESTIC DOGS

+ Excessive howling, or barking. (Problem 18)

● Dogs who are left free to roam will tend to form groups. These groups of dogs may run and hunt together and can go into a frenzy of killing if they get in amongst a herd of sheep who are in a confined area and cannot escape. (Problem 13A)

● We have observed that if two dogs get into a fight, other dogs in the area will be triggered to join in. This may be related to their attack behaviour on prey, one wolf taking a hold of the prey and others joining in. (Problem 12C)

● Dogs who live together may chase off a strange dog who enters their home area, see Agonistic behaviour.

Summary: Wolves live in a highly organised social group and keep close together for most of the time to enhance their prospects of survival. Dogs have inherited the need for a similar social structure.

8. Sexual behaviour

Looking for and finding a mate

Incomplete sexual behaviour may occur as early as three to four weeks of age when puppies sometimes mount and clasp one another, or an owner's arm or leg! We have noticed that dogs who constantly display this type of behaviour are often 'dominant' animals who exhibit a high level of bold behaviour. This agrees with the observations of people that have studied wolves in the wild who tell us that it is usually the more superior males and females of the pack who mate.

Puberty marks the time when males and females are able to mate. In dogs it usually occurs between six and nine months of age and is marked by the first heat in the female, and by leg lifting during urination in males. As discussed in Eliminative behaviour, leg lifting is not influenced by levels of the male hormone testosterone because dogs who are castrated prior to puberty also start to lift their legs at this age. However, testosterone does change the smell of a male dog's urine and other dogs will react to it accordingly. Male dogs are able to mate all year round until they are a ripe old age, whereas female dogs, with the exception of the Dingo and Basenji, usually come into season twice a year and are only receptive to mating for a short period of this time. The number of seasons is determined by the nutritional status of the bitch and the time of her seasons is influenced by the length of the days. She is more likely to give birth in spring or autumn.

The number of seasons per year and the age at which they start in the female dog contrasts markedly with the same features in female wolves, who begin

SEXUAL BEHAVIOUR

puberty between two and three *years* of age and only have one season per year. Presumably humans have selectively bred dogs to produce young at an earlier age, and more often. Earlier puberty may also be associated with a good food supply and the fact that many dog breeds are considerably smaller than wolves. Puberty usually results in a marked slowing of growth in various species including man.

Dingos and Basenjis only have one season a year.

When a female comes into season, or heat, she goes through four distinct phases:

1. *Pro-estrus* can be recognised when the vulva swells and drops of blood from the vagina appear on the floor. This discharge should not be confused with human menstruation which occurs *after* ovulation, as pro-estrus occurs *before* the bitch ovulates and is receptive to the male. It is caused by oozing of blood from small blood vessels in the uterus which is preparing for conception. Pro-estrus lasts for about nine days.

   Wolves indulge in a great deal of courtship behaviour during this time, including 'flirting' on the part of the female, but she will not allow the male to mate with her. She whirls around if he attempts to do so and either sits down or runs away enticing him to follow. This behaviour would certainly strengthen the bond between the two sexes.

2. *Estrus*, meaning frenzy, is the period when the female will 'stand' for the male; in fact she is a very active participant in the mating procedure. Ovulation occurs about the second day whether the female has mated or not. Estrus lasts for roughly nine days but may be extended if she does not mate, which presumably is nature's way of ensuring that she has the optimum chance of breeding. Detailed mating behaviour has not been observed in wolves in the wild, but captive wolves show similar behaviour to dogs. The female begins to flag her tail to the side when she is receptive and this action exposes her vagina. She will help the male in his efforts to mount her and a 'tie' is achieved when his penis swells in her vagina. The male will then turn around so that the pair face in opposite directions. Ejaculation takes place shortly after the tie but the pair may stay bonded together for up to thirty minutes. It is useless to try to separate a bitch and dog during this time, hoping that the bitch will not become pregnant, because ejaculation will already have taken place and you will only hurt both bitch and dog in the process. You should con-

sult a veterinarian *within 24 hours* if your bitch has been mated by mistake, as a resultant pregnancy can be prevented by hormone treatment. We will discuss how best to avoid such an occurrence in Problem 26.

Humans rarely allow two dogs to go through the normal courtship routine even if they wish the pair to mate, which may be another reason why male dogs are not usually interested in raising their offspring. All too frequently, male and female are brought together and expected to mate on demand. No wonder the process is sometimes unsuccessful! Dog owners occasionally utilise artificial insemination which may be beneficial from a genetic viewpoint, or practical if the dog and bitch live in different countries, but the litter is hardly the result of natural selection! People should be examining breeding practices carefully and reviewing what is being done to dogs by the creation of many breeds which are desperately inferior structurally to the natural wolf.

3. *Met estrus* is the time of pregnancy if the bitch has mated and conceived. It lasts for approximately sixty-three days. Whether she is pregnant or not, females undergo the same hormonal changes and they often experience a false, or pseudopregnancy. This can involve all the signs of a regular pregnancy and birth, such as loss of appetite, producing milk, mothering objects and becoming more aggressive about guarding her 'den'. It has been intimated that pseudopregnancy in wolves would help the pack to survive because non pregnant females would be physically capable of producing milk and helping to nurse the cubs. This would allow the more dominant mothers, who might be superior hunters, to go out and hunt with the pack, while the less dominant and less aggressive females stay in the den to 'baby-sit' and feed the litter.

4. *An-estrus* is the time of reproductive inactivity between seasons. Whelping or giving birth is not discussed in this book as any problems arising are physical rather than behavioural. You should consult your veterinarian immediately if problems arise.

POTENTIAL PROBLEMS RELATING TO SEXUAL BEHAVIOUR

IN DOMESTIC DOGS

● Males mounting or clasping other dogs or bitches.

+ Males mounting or clasping humans. (Problem 21)

● Increased territorial aggression in females when they have young pups. This is associated with care giving behaviour.

+ Male dogs congregating around the house of a bitch in heat. (Problem 26)

● Male dogs frustrated and distracted by a bitch in heat.

● A tendency for entire males to wander further from home, which gives them an increased chance of meeting a receptive bitch.

● Bitches wandering further afield during pro-estrus and estrus. (Problem 26)

+ Bitches being less receptive to their 'human' family during this period. (Problem 26)

+ Unwanted pregnancy and unwanted litter. (Problem 26)

Summary: Sexual behaviour is similar in wolves and dogs, but dogs are rarely allowed to express their sexuality naturally. Dogs have been selectively bred to produce young earlier in life and more frequently.

9. Care giving behaviour

Looking after the young and looking after yourself

The most obvious example of care giving in wolves and dogs is the attention they give to their young. It starts at birth when the mother chews through the foetal membrane and the umbilical cord and stimulates and dries the puppy by licking it. Licking the pups not only keeps them clean but stimulates urination and defecation. By licking up the resultant deposits, the bitch keeps the bed or den clean.

She feeds them by lying on one side and allowing them to suckle. If one pup becomes separated from the rest, she will pick it up by holding its body in her jaws with the feet dangling down and return it to the rest. This ensures that the pups are kept warm and safe. Bitches are often extremely protective of their young at this age.

When the pups are about three weeks old, mother wolves and some mother dogs start to vomit pre-digested food for them and gradually begin to wean

CARE GIVING BEHAVIOUR

them. Male wolves and older siblings also vomit food for the pups, a behaviour which is unlikely to be seen in male dogs, probably because of their lack of involvement in 'child' rearing.

Care giving behaviour in adult dogs who do not have a litter is mainly restricted to minor actions of self-care such as scratching an irritation, rubbing themselves on an upright object, rolling on the ground, biting at their coats, shaking after being in the water and grooming themselves, chiefly around the anal and genital region. They attempt to make themselves as comfortable as possible by circling around to check the ground underneath before they lie down, and readily dig a large hole in moist earth to keep cool during a hot spell.

Both wolves and dogs will lick at wounds on another animal, probably because the secretions are attractive in smell and taste rather than in a conscious effort to clean the area.

POTENTIAL PROBLEMS RELATED TO CARE GIVING BEHAVIOUR IN DOMESTIC DOGS

The first problem listed below would only be experienced by a dog breeder or someone visiting young pups, while the subsequent problems are frequently experienced by many owners.

● A bitch has a natural instinct to protect her pups, particularly in the early weeks. This may lead her to attack, threaten or bite other dogs, or unfamiliar people who come too close to them for her liking. The answer is so obvious that we are not going to deal with it in the problem section. We should respect the right of the bitch to guard her pups, at least until they are between two and three weeks old. After that time the pups should be handled by different people including gentle children and potential owners. If the bitch is still wary, she can be removed from the scene for a while and taken for a well earned walk.

● Many owners are faced with the problem of a dog which continuously scratches and bites at different parts of its body, usually around the rump or paws. There is often a physical reason for this, commonly fleas, an allergy, or infection caused by a grass seed. It is rarely a behavioural problem and advice should be sought from a veterinarian.

+ Compulsive licking. (Problem 17)

● Dogs commonly enjoy rolling in the most unmentionable substances!

● They often dig large holes in shady areas to keep cool. (Problem 15)

Summary: There is virtually no difference between the care giving behaviour of wolves and dogs, except that dogs are more likely to be subjected to the stress of strangers near their young pups. This may lead to defensive aggressive reactions.

CHAPTER 6 HOW DOGS COMMUNICATE

Dogs transmit information to each other in three important ways: by use of body language, by chemicals called pheronomes which they can smell and which are secreted by all dogs, and by sound.

1. Communication through body language

Body language is used to maintain harmonious relationships throughout a wolf group so that physical confrontation is kept to a minimum, see Chapter 5: Agonistic behaviour. Pups start to learn to read body language very early in life and, as a result a stable hierarchy can be established by the time they are only fifteen weeks old. If pups are reared alone or taken away from their litter too early, they may not be good at reading this social language and this will lead to an increased likelihood of aggression. This is just one of the reasons why it is better to leave pups in their litter until they are seven to eight weeks of age. When a pup is taken to its new home, usually when it is approximately eight weeks old, it is essential to continue socialising it with other healthy immunised pups, see Chapter 2: Socialise your puppy.

Dogs also become extremely good at reading human body language! When we hear people say 'Fido understands every word I say', what their dog is really doing is understanding many of the *movements* and *actions* the owners make! For instance, opening the fridge door may herald teatime, the clink of car keys may mean a walk, a certain outfit of clothing may mean the dog is going to be left alone while the owner goes to work. These are all fairly obvious signals to the dog. The words that accompany the actions mean little. However, sometimes dogs read extremely subtle signals which we don't even realise we are giving! At about 11 p.m. Ruth only needs to uncross her legs prior to standing up, and the dogs are on their feet and running to the door for their night-time outing. A horse, aptly named 'Clever Hans', was immortalised in Germany because he had all sorts of experts, and even his handler, tricked into thinking he could count and do sums! What his handler didn't realise was that the horse stopped tapping out numbers with his hoof when the handler raised his eyebrow very slightly as he reached the correct answer. 'Clever Hans' was indeed clever, but not in the way they thought.

We use verbal language in an extremely sophisticated way and our ability to do this makes us pay less attention to each other's body language. However, if you want to communicate effectively with your dog, it is most important that you learn what the canine postures mean. In Chapter 5, Agonistic behaviour, we explained that superior dogs tend to make themselves look larger and inferior ones, smaller. Let's look at that in a bit more detail. Observe the position of the head, ears, hair, tail and the body position. The photographs show some examples.

The **resting dog** has its ears and tail relaxed and its hair lying flat on its body, whether it is lying down, sitting or standing.

The **alert dog** stands with ears and head erect and its hair lying flat on its body.

THE ALERT DOG

The **aggressive dog** stands with its ears, tail, hackles and rump hair erect to make itself look more imposing.

THE AGGRESSIVE DOG

The **highly aggressive dog** stands with its ears, tail, hackles and rump hair erect and, in addition, it snarls or growls, exposing its teeth, and tends to move forwards.

The **hunting** or **herding dog** moves with its head held low and keeps a fixed stare on its 'prey' in preparation for a rush. If the 'prey' does not run as the dog approaches, then the dog's head will come up to a more normal level.

THE HERDING DOG

The **playful dog** exhibits a wide repertoire of behaviour from barking and licking to dancing and twirling around. It may extend its forelegs forward and lower its head to the ground in the characteristic play bow attitude while wagging its tail gently. Its ears will be up and its hair lies flat on its body. It will often leap sideways in an effort to get you, or another dog, to join in a game!

THE PLAY BOW

PLAYFUL BEHAVIOUR. NOTE THE RELAXED LEGS AND THE FACT THAT BOTH DOGS LOOK BOLD.

The **fearful** or **stressed dog** has its ears back and its tail between its legs.

THE FEARFUL DOG

The **very fearful dog** cringes down low with its tail firmly tucked under its body.

The **submissive** or **inferior dog** lies on its side with one hind leg elevated and it may urinate.

NOTE: It is very important never to punish a dog for urinating, especially when it is in this position. In canine terms this dog is saying, 'I give in, please back off.' If you punish a dog in this situation, you contravene canine law, and make the dog even more fearful and likely to urinate again.

THE SUBMISSIVE DOG

After examining the signs which dogs give to signal their intentions you can understand why some dogs may misunderstand the body language of other dogs because of their excessive hair, especially around the eyes or neck, or if they have docked tails. We mentioned in Chapter 4 that fluffy dogs seem to be attacked more frequently, perhaps because they look as if their hackles are raised.

Dogs which look like their ancestor, the wolf, have pricked ears and this may make it easier for other dogs to read them accurately. Conversely, it is possible that dogs with floppy juvenile-type ears are less likely to be attacked because they look more puppy-like.

Dogs are not often lucky enough to live in a stable group such as a wolf pack, so they have to cope with many extra stresses such as meeting up with strange dogs of all shapes and sizes. The differences in ear carriage, tail length, shape of face, length of hair and prominence of the eyes all confuse the issue and make it more difficult for dogs to read each other's body language! The wolf, after all, only has to read an image similar to itself.

Small dogs don't seem to realise that they are small! A Chihuahua will exhibit more or less the same behaviours as a Great Dane, and will sometimes challenge a much larger animal. To draw an analogy, imagine a six foot man coming up against someone five times as tall! It's a wonder that small dogs don't get into trouble more often; a tribute to the dogs' social structure and the functioning of appropriate body language.

Let's now imagine ourselves in a typical suburban situation and put the knowledge we have learnt about canine body language into practice. We are assuming your dog has no behaviour problems, that you walk it in a safe environment free from traffic and that it has been taught to come when it is called. If your dog does not come when called then you must teach it to do this first (Exercise 1). Sometimes it is better to visit the same park at the same time each day so that you get to know both the dogs and owners who walk there, especially if you are an inexperienced dog handler. We recommend that you walk your dog off lead. If this is not permitted by law, then use a very long lead of about 5 metres and keep it slack.

Let's look at the clues that tell us that another dog is likely to cause a confrontation. The clues come from both the dogs and their handlers.

NOTE: The following advice must always be tempered with common sense. Be particularly careful when two entire male dogs meet.

1. If a dog is running free in the park with its owner, it is unlikely to cause a problem. Continue to give your dog its freedom.

2. Dogs who are roaming free on their own rarely initiate aggression because they come into contact with so many dogs that they socialise themselves! Continue to give your dog freedom.

3. Groups of two or more dogs may act like a pack and can be intimidating to a single dog. Give your dog freedom but monitor the situation carefully. Move away from the group and call your dog away the moment mutual investigation has taken place.

4. Dogs who are being walked on leads are usually restricted for three reasons, firstly because they might run away, secondly because the owner knows their dog is aggressive and thirdly because they think your dog might be aggressive. Call out to the owner and find out the situation. If their dog is not aggressive, suggest that they let it off lead to play with yours provided that their dog will come back when called. You and your dog may both find a new friend!

5. Dogs who hide behind their owners are generally fearful and may rush and snap at your dog. They rarely do any damage; however, such behaviour could trigger an aggressive response from your own dog. Call your dog to you and avoid passing too close to this type of dog or you will only stress it more.

6. If you meet a dog which is known to be aggressive, or looks aggressive, do the obvious; call your dog to you and move a substantial distance away

from the offending dog. Do not restrain your dog on lead unless absolutely necessary. It's not your dog that is the problem!

7. Never go close to a dog which is tied up or lying close to someone's possessions. It may lunge at you, either because it is restrained or because it is conditioned to be aggressive when someone goes close to its owners belongings.

2. *Communication through scent*

Dogs also communicate by smelling pheronomes in each other's urine, faeces, saliva and vaginal and anal secretions, a method of communication which we cannot share! These chemical messages give a very accurate picture of the dog's status, whether it is male or female, and sexually receptive or not. Urine is one of the major sources of pheronomes and is a vital form of individual identification, along with secretions from the anal glands. Male dogs frequently scratch the ground after they have defecated, which makes an additional visual marker for other dogs, and also spreads pheronomes secreted by sweat glands between the paws onto the ground. Humans also secrete pheronomes which is the reason why many dogs like to pick up unwashed underwear and socks and carrry them in their mouths!

COMMUNICATION THROUGH SCENT

3. *Communication through sound*

Unlike humans, the dog's weakest form of communication is through sound. Tuned as we are to listen to one another, we quickly learn to interpret what our dog's vocalisations mean. Most owners recognise the sound that means 'I want in/out', 'There's someone at the door', or 'It hurts!'

Young pups cry and mew well before their own ear canals are open. Crying leads to milk let-down in the bitch, a feeling which most human mothers will have experienced.

Barking is sometimes used by wolves as a warning mechanism, but domestic dogs bark much more frequently because they are exposed to a greater variety of noises. Howling is a method of bringing the pack together after a hunt, or of letting one wolf know where others are. When one wolf howls, the others join in. In a similar way, when one dog howls, the whole street may join the chorus. Sirens or highly pitched music may bring about a similar response.

The yelp is a characteristic response to pain or fright.

Dogs often learn to respond to humans in a different way from other dogs, usually because we reinforce the behaviour, sometimes unknowingly. Our Golden Retriever moans through her nose when she is

COMMUNICATION THROUGH SOUND

scratched under the chin or when her favourite food is around. Adult dogs frequently whine to gain our attention but rarely make this sound to other dogs.

Given all this information, we can conclude that dogs can communicate extremely effectively with one another, provided they have the chance to learn the rules. In fact, they usually signal their intentions more clearly than people! If we take the trouble to observe them as carefully as they observe us, we can experience the immense pleasure of understanding the behaviour of another species. We can also help our dog to live harmoniously in suburbia.

CHAPTER 7 HOW DOGS LEARN

Imagine how a young wolf or a dog learns. It goes out exploring its environment, wandering around and using its senses to expand its knowledge of different sights, smells, tastes, noises, and textures. It hears a rustling in the undergrowth. It smells a warm body. Suddenly it sees a small hairy animal scurrying along the ground. The dog gives chase and quickly kills the little animal. Eating the animal is highly beneficial and necessary for survival.

In this scene we can identify what psychologists call the stimulus, the response, and the reinforcement.

The Stimulus	= the rustling of the animal (stimulates the sense of hearing)
	= the odour of the warm body (stimulates the sense of smell)
	= the sight of the animal scurrying along (stimulates the sense of sight)
The Response	= the dog giving chase
The Reinforcement	= the food which is eaten after the kill

As a result when that dog experiences a similar stimulus again (the rustling, the odour and the movement of the little animal), then it is likely to respond in the same way by giving chase and killing, because it has been reinforced for its response in the past by eating its kill.

In the same way, if we stimulate a puppy to come to us when it is called by offering it a hand and voice signal, and we then reinforce its response by giving it a piece of food, the puppy will quickly learn that coming to us on these signals is highly beneficial. In other words, the reinforcement will create and maintain the puppy's habit of coming to us when it is called. This process is known as **operant conditioning**.

Reinforcement

We have just seen that reinforcement will create and maintain habits. Professor B. F. Skinner, a well known Harvard psychologist who carried out numerous experiments on how animals learn, observed that there were two kinds of reinforcement.

(a) **Positive reinforcement** adds something which is of benefit to an animal or human, e.g. giving a dog a piece of meat after a desirable response, eating the kill after a chase, patting the dog after a response or giving it the opportunity to retrieve something.

(b) **Negative reinforcement** takes away something which is unpleasant to an animal or human, e.g. if a person jerks a dog in the neck with a choker chain when it pulls ahead during a walk, then the subsequent slackening of the chain when the dog does not pull is negatively reinforcing to the dog.

Postive reinforcement can be divided into two further categories:

Primary reinforcement or primary reinforcers are benefits which are essential for survival, e.g. food or water. *They have an extremely powerful effect on behaviour.*

In human terms a primary reinforcer may be the money we get paid for doing a job. This enables us to buy food and drink, and pay the mortgage or rent, etc.; in other words, to survive.

Secondary reinforcers are benefits which only reinforce behaviour because they have been paired with a primary reinforcer on a number of occasions, e.g. if a dog responds by coming to us on signal and we reinforce it by giving it a piece of food and, at the same time, say 'good boy', then the words 'good boy' will eventually become a reinforcement in its own right.

Secondary reinforcers are much less powerful as a means of influencing behaviour and they must continue to be paired with a primary reinforcer occasionally to keep up their effect. In human terms, we would be unlikely to work for a boss who patted us on the back at the end of each week, but who only paid us once a year!

THE RELATIVE EFFECTIVENESS OF VARIOUS TYPES OF REINFORCEMENT AS A MEANS OF TEACHING DOGS OR MODIFYING PROBLEM BEHAVIOURS

Dogs, like us, are reinforced by many things in life: a ball to chase, a game of tug of war, the opportunity to go for a walk, being patted, lying near the fire on a cool night, playing with other dogs, chasing cars and digging holes. The list goes on and on. However, none of the things mentioned above is as powerful as the use of a primary reinforcer like food as a means of influencing behaviour.

Patting and food are two positive reinforcers which are commonly used in dog training. Set up a little experiment for yourself using a dog with a normal healthy appetite. Place the dog between two people who are standing 4 metres apart. Ask one person to call the dog and pat it when it comes to them. Ask the other to give the dog a piece of its favourite food when it comes to them. The result is a foregone conclusion; the dog will quickly learn to respond to the person who reinforces it for coming with a piece of food and ignore the person who reinforces it with pats. The reason? Food equals survival, patting does not.

So we can logically conclude that patting is an inefficient way of reinforcing a dog's behaviour.

Of course the effects of any reinforcement depends upon the way we feel at the time. After a walk, a dog may be reinforced more by lying down by the fire than by going for another walk. A millionaire will not be motivated to work for $10! Likewise a dog will be less motivated by food immediately after a large meal. However, we have already seen in Chapter 5: Ingestive behaviour, that wolves spend much of their waking lives looking for food. Any normal dog will exhibit the same behaviour given the opportunity unless it is being fed too much or too frequently. In fact, we humans also spend much of our time in the pursuit of food but in rather less direct ways. Instead of hunting, we work to earn money which in turn buys food for us and our families. The survival urge is strong in all animals. So we can conclude that food is a natural motivator and a natural, highly efficient form of reinforcement.

THE EFFECTS OF PRIMARY REINFORCERS SUCH AS FOOD ON A DOG'S BEHAVIOUR

Food is used in this example as it is the most efficient convenient form of positive reinforcement.

1. The dog will learn quickly and willingly as it is never forced to do anything, i.e. it produces voluntary responses. Usually six to twelve repetitions are necessary to produce or condition a habit. To maintain a habit, we simply need to reinforce the response occasionally with food.
2. The relationship between the dog and the handler will be excellent because the dog associates training, and the handler, with the great benefit of food.
3. The dog develops and maintains an excellent temperament because it is never exposed to punishment. It will be bold and outgoing as a result.
4. A great number of responses can be conditioned in a short time and at a young age, e.g. coming when called, sitting, standing, dropping, staying and heeling can be taught in a matter of minutes!
5. Problem behaviours can be modified rapidly by substituting the problem behaviour with an alternative behaviour which is acceptable to us, and then reinforcing the new behaviour with food.

Punishment

The term 'negative reinforcement' describes the removal of something unpleasant. Logically this implies that if something is to be negatively reinforc- ing to an animal, then something nasty or aversive must precede it.

Anything which is aversive is called a punishment.

MATES FOR LIFE

Experiments have shown that punishment in animals is only effective in two circumstances. Firstly, the punishment must be meted out during, or immediately after, the event. Secondly, the punishment must be severe if it is to have any lasting impact or effect, e.g. if the small hairy animal we spoke of at the beginning of this chapter had turned around and attacked the dog, inflicting severe injuries, then the dog would be unlikely to chase that type of animal again. Instead, it would become extremely fearful and avoid that type of animal at all costs in the future. This mechanism is necessary in the wild to ensure survival. However, it is never necessary, or wise, to subject domestic dogs to this type of aversive event in order to modify their behaviour. Punishing experiences

such as this have many undesirable side effects which are detailed further on in this chapter.

Unfortunately, many dog owners do not think of the use of correction chains or forcing the dog into position as punishment. They imagine that it has similar implications to marking a child's homework with a cross to indicate an incorrect answer. However, a teacher can usually explain verbally and visually how to arrive at the correct response, but dogs cannot understand this type of explanation. Instead they are physically manipulated to respond in the way that the handler desires and anything which is forced on a human or animal is aversive, in other words it is a punishment.

THE EFFECTS OF PUNISHMENT SUCH AS THE USE OF A CORRECTION CHAIN ON A DOG'S BEHAVIOUR

1. Mild to moderate punishment, such as a jerk on the neck with a correction chain followed by negative reinforcement in the form of the chain going slack, will teach a dog to respond after a *considerable* number of repetitions. However, the severity of the jerk to the neck will have to be gradually increased to maintain the dog's response. We can therefore conclude that this is an inefficient method of teaching.
2. The animal responds because it has to, not because it wants to, i.e. it produces involuntary responses.
3. Punishment creates a fear response which dramatically reduces the dog's ability to learn new things.
4. It spoils the social relationship between the dog which is being punished, and the person who is inflicting the punishment.

NOTE: It is a popular misconception that correction is a necessary component of teaching. Punishment in the form of correction is never necessary if a dog has been taught desirable responses in the first place. Nor is punishment needed when modifying a problem behaviour.

After you have examined the evidence about the relative merits of various types of reinforcement and the effects of reinforcement and punishment on a dog's behaviour, we are sure you will come to the same conclusion as we have done. Numerous experiments conducted by psychologists and animal behaviourists have shown that positive reinforcement is infinitely more effective and humane than the use of punishment and negative reinforcement. Of the two positive reinforcers commonly used in dog training, food and patting, food is much more efficient because it is a primary reinforcer necessary for survival. For this reason, you will find that we use food as a means of reshaping problem behaviour and reinforcing acceptable alternative behaviour throughout this book.

In one of his last written statements Professor Skinner said, **'anyone who remains satisfied with punishment without exploring nonpunitive alternatives is making a real mistake'.** We are in complete agreement with him.

Shaping or re-shaping behaviour

There are many people who are against the use of food when training dogs because they do not know how to use it in a scientific way. Food is used in two ways:

1. **To shape or re-shape behaviour** (using classical conditioning)
   Food is held in the hand as part of the *stimulus* to get the dog into the desired position, e.g. if you place your right hand, containing food, in front of your dog's nose and then raise this hand directly above the dog's head, it will tend to look up and fall into the sit position. As this happens, you give the voice signal 'sit' and then reinforce the dog by giving it the piece of food.

   This should only need to be repeated six to a dozen times before the dog will respond to the voice and hand signals *without* food in the hand.
2. **To reinforce behaviour** (using operant conditioning)
   The dog is given food after it has responded to the voice and hand signal, e.g. when it goes into the sit position.

Professor B. F. Skinner did numerous experiments on schedules of reinforcement to find out how to maintain an animal's response at the most efficient level. He found that the ones who responded and remembered their lessons best were the ones who were reinforced *intermittently*, ie. they could not predict when they would be fed.

It is just like the way people behave with gambling machines. They keep putting money in the slot and pulling the lever in the hope that the machine will respond by regurgitating money! If they never win, they soon give up gambling. If they win occasionally, they tend to keep responding by putting more money in the slot! It's not only dogs that respond to intermittent reinforcement.

You will see how to put all this theory into practice when we show you how to teach your dog to come every time it is called (Exercise 1).

CHAPTER 8 DOG BEHAVIOURAL PROBLEMS: AN INTRODUCTION

The solutions to the problems that we talk about throughout this book largely depend on common sense combined with a thorough knowledge of the dog's natural behaviours and senses, years of practical experience and a genuine desire to see the 'problem' from a canine perspective. We will show you how to cure problems by using proven scientific behavioural modification techniques as explained in Chapter 7, which we have adapted to the treatment of dogs.

Every problem that we address in this book comes with a very clear message. Dog problems are caused by humans! We create an unnatural environment for dogs and we often have little understanding of their needs. Our expectations are frequently unrealistic!

It is essential when we look at a dog problem that we understand it from the dog's point of view. The secret to modifying the problem is to produce an alternative behaviour which we find acceptable, and which the dog *prefers* to do.

The new behaviour should make the problem behaviour impossible, e.g. if a dog jumps up on people, we should stimulate it to sit and then reinforce the sit response with food. The dog will find it more beneficial to sit, than to jump all over us. In turn, we are reinforced for solving the problem which makes us more likely to behave in the same way in the future. A kind of happy 'Catch 22' situation!

NOTE: There are a number of key exercises which are constantly recommended throughout this book. The recall, sit at side, heel off lead, sit stay and the retrieving exercise have been grouped in one section near the back for your convenience.

Problems

LIFE IN THE BALANCE

PROBLEM 1 BOREDOM
— THE MOST FREQUENT CAUSE OF PROBLEMS

CAUSE

The very act of restricting a dog to our back garden for long periods of time is the reason for most of the behavioural problems we develop in it. Ironically, dogs kept by less caring owners who allow them to roam the streets, develop few of the problems we discuss in this book. Without restriction, these dogs come and go as they please, enjoying all the benefits that freedom permits. They rarely hang on the washing, dig holes or develop the countless problems that result from boredom and confinement.

However, we are obviously not advising you to let your dog roam unattended. The motor car could soon claim it as another of its many victims.

Boredom is caused by the fact that the domestic dog is not normally able to express itself as nature intended, because its behaviours are either repressed or totally prohibited. How would you feel if you were left at home all day, every day, with no one to talk to, no television to watch, no books to read, no work to do and no opportunity to exercise? It would be worse than being in prison. The two most serious ways in which we limit our dog's quality of life is by restricting its opportunity to investigate its environment and by denying it social contact. Therefore most of the solutions to boredom-related 'misbehaviour' attempt to remedy these two important problems.

+ Most dogs lack the opportunity to move around and explore naturally.

+ Dogs are frequently not even permitted to eliminate in preferred spots, to scent mark or to smell the deposits that other dogs have left behind.

+ They are not allowed to hunt for their own food.

+ They are often deprived of regular social contact with other dogs. During the day, their human 'family' is frequently away at work or school. Many dogs are not even allowed in the house to be part of the family.

+ For obvious reasons, most dogs are not encouraged to find a mate, to breed, or raise pups.

PREVENTION AND CURE

1. Walk your dog at least once a day, preferably more, for at least half an hour. Elderly or toy dogs may require a little less.

2. Your dog should be exercised off lead wherever possible, as long as it is in no danger from traffic. This allows it to investigate naturally, to use all its senses and to do all the things that dogs enjoy.

   Some people seem to think that a ride in the car is enough to keep a dog amused, but it certainly is not!

3. Use a long lead of 3 to 4 metres in length when you cannot walk your dog off lead. This will allow the dog to sniff and explore over a reasonable area. It will have the added benefit of minimising the likelihood of the dog learning to pull on the lead. Most dogs pull to get to scent posts and other things of canine interest. Short leads do not allow them to do this.

4. Try to go to different parks and walking areas so that your dog visits a variety of places. This is not absolutely essential as dogs seem to find different things to investigate every day, even if they are taken to the same place. However, most dogs do enjoy a change and seem to be stimulated by it.

5. Train your dog regularly to give it some 'work' to do. Training also establishes control over your dog and allows you to call the dog back to you whenever you wish, an essential response when dogs are given their freedom off lead.

6. Your dog should have regular contact with other dogs while they are all off lead. Dogs will behave much more normally if they are not restricted and leads can trigger aggressive responses.

7. Play with your dog regularly. This not only benefits the dog but you too! Watching a dog enjoying itself is one of the most satisfying things on earth!

If you go out to work, the following suggestions are particularly important but, even if you are at

BROOK WITH FRIENDS

BROOK AT WORK

BROOK AT PLAY

home all day, some of them will make your dog's life more fulfilling.

8. You may find that feeding your dog in the morning is beneficial, because it will be more likely to sleep for a while after its meal while you are at work and less likely to indulge in undesirable behaviour!

   If you give your dog a large marrowbone occasionally, it will be much less likely to chew on other things while you are away.

9. Take your dog to work with you if at all possible. Our dogs have been a great success in a centre which Ruth attends where they visit elderly and disabled people. We use them for socialising with dog 'clients', especially those who are a little nervous. Our dogs also take part in lectures and demonstrations and attend dog club once a week, so they have a fairly varied life at 'work' as well as at play.

10. Perhaps your dog could be left with a friend or relative who is home during the day.

11. Alternatively, you could arrange for a neighbour or friend to visit the dog occasionally and perhaps take it for a walk. This might suit a responsible child who is not allowed a pet of their own. Professional dog walkers are available in some cities.

12. Careful consideration should be given to putting a doggy door (Problem 18) somewhere in the house, so that the dog can go in and out whenever it chooses. It does not need to have the run of the house, entry into the kitchen is sufficient. Although this can cause a problem with dirt in wet weather, that problem is minute compared with the types of problems which can be solved by a doggy door. You can leave a strip of carpet or paper on either side of the door to absorb moisture from wet paws.

BROOK AT REST

13. We strongly believe that *all* dogs should be allowed in the house when their owners are at home. After all, we have taken the dogs away from their litters and it is *our* responsibility to provide a substitute for the natural social contact which they have lost. If your dog is very excitable when it is in the house, this excitement will die down quickly once the dog realises that it is there to stay. You can create the behaviour you want by training the dog in the house and reinforcing passive responses such as the 'sit stay' (Exercise 3). It is up to you to decide how much freedom your dog should have in the house. Our dogs are not restricted because that is the way we like it but, as long as you are consistent, your dog will soon realise where it can go and where it cannot.

14. We have no evidence to suggest that dogs are calmed by a radio or television which has been left on for their benefit. However, the noise may mask other sounds such as barking dogs, which can trigger unwanted activity in your dog. You could try it anyway!

15. You should consider getting a companion for your dog. We have two dogs and so do many of our friends. Watching them play together is a great source of amusement and laughter. However, a companion should not be seen as a panacea for all ills. Sometimes dogs don't get along and sometimes they can spell double trouble! You could offer to look after a friend's dog for a few days and see what happens.

A second dog should certainly not be regarded as a cure for the first dog's behavioural problems, nor is it a substitute for regular exercise and plenty of human company and attention. How to introduce a second dog into the household for the first time is explained in Problem 24.

Investigatory   Ingestive   Eliminative   Care Seeking   Shelter Seeking   Agonistic

PROBLEM 2 NOT COMING WHEN CALLED

– 'THE RECALL' IS THE BASIS FOR CONTROL

The problem of the dog that won't come when it is called is surprisingly common and very frustrating for the owner, but relatively easy to solve.

CAUSE

● Dogs naturally want to explore their surroundings as this allows them to hunt and survive in the wild.

● Their sense of smell is highly developed and they may be distracted by odours which humans do not even realise exist.

+ + They are easily triggered into chasing fast moving objects.

NOTE: Often dog owners inadvertently teach their dogs *not* to come when called by calling 'come' when the dog is busy investigating elsewhere, e.g. sniffing the neighbour's dog. As a result the dog begins to associate the signal 'come' not with coming to you, but with a completely different behaviour, that is, sniffing the neighbour's dog!

+ Many dogs are punished when they eventually return to their owners after running away. Naturally enough, the punishment only makes the dog even more unwilling to return the next time! It will be much more likely to run off to investigate people and objects which *benefit* it.

● Dogs have a strong desire to be part of a group. They can become highly excited by the presence of other dogs, particularly if they have limited opportunities to play and socialise.

PREVENTION AND CURE

1. Teach the 'recall', as shown overleaf, in a restricted environment such as your house or the back garden, making sure that your dog is really keen for its food reinforcement before you begin. If your dog is not motivated by food you should postpone its meal for a few hours and train it just before it eats.

2. Progress to practising the recall exercise in different situations, such as the park, where there are distractions. Dogs can suffer from a phenomenon known as 'stimulus dis-  (Continued on page 57.)

FRUSTRATION!

THE *Recall* EXERCISE
■NITIAL CONDITIONING

1. Wait until your dog is looking at you from a short distance away.

2. Move away from your dog to encourage it to come towards you, and drop your hand low to the ground. At this stage your hand should have food in it. You can use either your right or left hand, whichever is more comfortable, but usually the right hand is used.

3. Say, 'come', once only when your dog is actually moving towards you.

4. Reinforce your dog with the piece of food in your hand the moment it reaches you.

5. Remove your hand quickly away up to your waist level.

6. Repeat points 1–5 until the dog's behaviour becomes predictable, i.e. conditioned. This should not take more than a dozen repetitions.

Investigatory   Ingestive   Eliminative   Care Seeking   Shelter Seeking   Agonistic

Maintain Conditioning

Once the dog's behaviour is predictable and it always comes to you on signal you should do the following to maintain its response:

1. Stop using food in the hand to help to stimulate a response.
2. The hand signal must remain the same whether there is food in the hand or not. Dogs can detect very subtle variations in hand signals.
3. It shouldn't be necessary to move away from your dog unless it is responding slowly.
4. The food which you are going to use as a reinforcer should be kept in a pocket or pouch where the dog cannot see it.
5. It is essential that you stop reinforcing your dog every time it responds correctly; however, do not make the intervals between reinforcers (the food) too long to begin with, e.g. reinforce the second, fifth, first, fourth or sixth response, choosing the quickest responses to reinforce.

Your reinforcement must become unpredictable so the dog does not know when it will be fed.

The difference between initial conditioning and maintaining conditioning should now be clear.

INITIAL CONDITIONING	MAINTAINING CONDITIONING
The Stimulus	
(a) Your movement away from the dog. (b) Your hand signal low to the ground. (c) Your verbal signal 'come'. (d) The food in your hand.	(a) Your hand signal low to the ground. (b) Your verbal signal 'come'. NOTE: No food to induce the response.
The Response	
The dog is *induced* to come in response to the above stimuli.	The dog *comes* in response to the above stimuli.
The Reinforcement	
The food given to the dog from your *hand*.	The food given to the dog **intermittently** from your *pocket*.

crimination' which means that they respond in one environment, but not in another! We know plenty of backyard Rin Tin Tins that happily ignore their owners in the park! This can be cured by simply going back to initial conditioning procedures in a more restricted environment and building up to the big exciting world outside. Make sure your dog is *truly* motivated by the food you use as an inducement and reinforcement.

3. Take your dog for daily walks off lead so that it has plenty of opportunity to investigate naturally.

4. *Never* punish your dog if it does not return to you immediately. Again, go back to initial conditioning, then maintain your dog's behaviour by continuing to reinforce it intermittently.

5. Consider training your dog to do many different exercises such as those shown in our first book *Dog Training: The Gentle Modern Method*. This will occupy your dog and give you confidence in your ability as a dog trainer.

PROBLEM 3 JUMPING UP

It is unusual to see dogs jumping up on each other as an expression of happiness. They usually mouth each other, run around bumping one another or roll over.

CAUSE

✚ ✚ The act of jumping up at a human being is taught or conditioned by people in the first place! Take, for example, the time when an eight week old puppy is being introduced into the family. There is much clapping of hands and bending of knees. The puppy runs to the person and climbs up using its front paws to reach the clapping hands, whereupon it is reinforced with physical and verbal praise. After a few repetitions of this act the puppy is conditioned to become an excellent jumping dog!

At first this jumping is of little consequence. Who cares, it's only a cute little puppy with tiny toes. Six months later 'cutie' now takes on the appearance of a baby elephant with kangaroo blood!

KANGAROO DOG!

✚ Unconsciously children often develop many desirable behaviours in dogs, but jumping is not one of them! Children who run around with their hands held up high make jumping all the more exciting for their dog!

✚ ✚ Dogs that perpetually jump at the back door, thereby scratching the paintwork or glass, are conditioned to do this by a number of different factors. After spending many boring hours on its own in the garden, a dog will be highly excited by the appearance of a familiar face at the back door. Dogs cannot clap their paws or say it's lovely to see you, they can only express their pleasure in a doggy way.

Secondly, dogs are often fed near the back door so the presence of their owners carrying food stimulates the jumping behaviour close to the door.

Thirdly, the sounds of excited children running to the door can trigger lively responses in a dog. So, too, can the rattle of a dog lead just prior to 'walk' time.

✚ Adults often hang over their dogs with their hands held out defensively at chest level when they expect their dog to leap up at them. The gesture in itself acts as a trigger to the dog to do more of the same! This may be further encouraged by the handler pushing the dog down to the ground. The game of 'I jump at you, then you push me down' is great fun for the dog!

The jumping dog problem can reach a point where children, and even adults, are too stressed by the dog's exuberance to venture out into the garden. Some of these dogs become chained up prisoners, others are reformed by the use of harsh, even cruel, methods: stamping on their rear feet, painfully squeezing their front paws, kneeing them in the chest or giving them a karate style chop across the nose. These belligerent actions are usually accompanied with gruff words such as 'get down' or 'bad dog'. When knowledge runs out, aggression hastens in.

Investigatory Ingestive Eliminative Care Seeking Shelter Seeking Agonistic

PREVENTION

If you have just acquired a puppy or are thinking of getting one, then preventive measures are quite simple. All you have to do is avoid promoting the jumping behaviour in the situations where it is most likely to occur, namely:

(a) When the pup runs to greet you.

(b) When you pat or stroke it.

(c) When it is likely to jump up at furniture, e.g. when you are sitting on a chair.

(d) When you open a door or gate.

(e) When you pick up its food bowl.

(f) When you carry toys or articles above its head.

(g) When children play with the puppy and throw their hands up high in excitement.

CURE

a, b, c & d

1. As the dog approaches you for whatever reason, place your hand containing a piece of food at the dog's nose level. Reinforce it in the stand position and then move your hand quickly away.

2. Repeat this action a number of times giving the same hand signal, but gradually offering food intermittently rather than every time.

NOTE: Do not dangle your hands above the dog's head as this will only generate more jumping problems!

e & f

Teach the 'sit' and 'sit stay' as shown in Exercises 2 and 3.

g

Encourage children to move around with their hands held low offering bits of food to the dog from time to time when all its four feet are on the ground. Make sure that the children are old enough and sensible enough to do this.

The problem of the dog that jumps up at doors or windows can be solved easily by putting in a doggy door (Problem 18) so that the dog has free access to the house. Alternatively you can place an object such as an open wooden box in front of the door to dissuade the dog from jumping.

THE TIME OF MY LIFE

Investigatory   Ingestive   Eliminative   Care Seeking   Shelter Seeking   Agonistic

PROBLEM 4 PULLING ON THE LEAD
– TEACH HEELING

CAUSE

+ All dogs have an inherited need to investigate their surroundings which would help them to survive in the wild, but this instinct is thwarted when a dog is placed on a lead. It quickly learns to pull so that it can sniff scent posts, etc. Puppies are not used to being restrained and often fight the lead, chew it, or lie down in a submissive way. Older dogs are stronger and can sometimes pull so hard that the owner finds it impossible to control them and stops taking them out. A vicious circle can result with lack of exercise leading to boredom-related misbehaviour which makes the dog even harder to control!

We have a friend, an ex-client, whose dog pulled so hard on the lead that she crashed into a tree, broke two of her teeth and ended up with an enormous dental bill! Fortunately for her active powerful dog, her response was to seek professional help from David, not to have the dog destroyed as some people might

have done. The offender has lost none of his mischief, but he is now a delightful receptive dog.

A great range of devices have been developed in an attempt to physically minimise the effect of dogs pulling on the lead. These range from the relatively new head halter to the dreaded correction chain which has been around since the last century, and which should die an overdue death as soon as possible. Numerous dogs have suffered cervical spine injuries from its inappropriate and zealous use, not to mention the emotional stress which is caused. At the same time, the unfortunate dog is often subjected to harsh verbal reprimands or whacked on the nose with a stick if it moves out in front of the handler.

The secret of a successful cure for this problem is similar to all the solutions in this book. You must give the dog a reason to *want* to walk beside you instead of pulling ahead.

PULLING LIKE A TRAIN!

CURE

1. First make sure your dog will come when called so that it is under control (Exercise 1). Then, teach your dog to heel beside you *off the lead* as shown opposite, so that it becomes conditioned to walk beside you without being restrained. Putting a lead on some dogs actually acts as a trigger to pull and can make it more difficult to shape the correct behaviour.

2. Once your dog has learnt to heel beside you off the lead, it is a simple matter to produce the same response on the lead.

   We suggest that you acquire a long light lead which you can clip onto your dog's fixed collar. Put the other end of the lead into your left-hand pocket, allowing a distinct loop to form between you and the dog. This will teach you not to use the lead as a restraint. Then condition your dog to heel as if it were off the lead by offering the same hand and voice signals and reinforcing the desired response intermittently. Later you can take the lead out of your pocket and hold it in a more conventional manner.

   At no time should the lead be used as a forceful training aid. It should only be used to ensure your dog's safety or to comply with local or government regulations.

PROBLEM RESOLVED

3. Having taught your dog to walk quietly beside you on the lead, you can then relax and allow your dog limited opportunities to explore at the end of a 3 to 4 metre long lead. After all, we don't want to turn an enjoyable walk into a military exercise! In congested areas you can go back to the more formal way of heeling so that the lead doesn't get tangled round someone's legs.

| Investigatory | Ingestive | Eliminative | Care Seeking | Shelter Seeking | Agonistic |

THE *Heel off Lead* EXERCISE
INITIAL CONDITIONING

This exercise requires excellent timing on the part of the handler. Unlike stationary exercises, such as the sit, your dog will move with you into a constantly changing environment with all its distractions. In order to compete with these distractions you must give clear and meaningful signals and reinforce the dog when it is in the correct position close to your left leg. It may help if you begin to teach this exercise in a long, narrow passageway, using this environment to help you shape the right response. It is important, however, never to crowd the dog when you do this.

1. Start with your dog at your left-hand side. Carry several pieces of food in your left hand and a piece in your right hand. Both hands should be held at waist level.

2. Step off with your left leg, simultaneously sweeping your right hand forward parallel to your dog at its eye level.

3. As your dog moves forward say 'heel'.

4. Move your right hand back to waist level as you take three to four brisk paces.

5. After three to four paces, stop your dog by placing your right hand in front of its nose, and reinforce it instantly.

6. Take another piece of food in your right hand and repeat points 2–5 a number of times.

NOTE: It is most important that you reinforce your dog when it is close to your left leg, and not when it is lagging behind you or surging ahead.

Maintain conditioning in the usual way by eliminating food as a stimulus and gradually increase the heeling distance literally step by step. It is best if you give short enjoyable lessons measured by the distance covered rather than the amount of time spent in training. Three or four heeling routines, each of twenty to thirty paces, is ample. If you multiply this by three or four training sessions per week you will have walked more than 400 metres in the heeling position. Enough to make Rin Tin Tin look inadequate!

PROBLEM 5 THE BIG SNIFFERS!

CAUSE

● As we know, the dog's sense of smell is vastly superior to our own; in fact it is really beyond our comprehension. It is natural for all dogs to sniff, but there are some breeds such as Bassets, Beagles and Bloodhounds whose noses seem to be glued to the ground. Once on a trail they can become oblivious to the rest of the world including their frustrated owner! This is a particular problem for people who want to show their dogs or take part in obedience trials.

● Other owners suffer the embarrassment of a dog that likes to sniff visitors in the crotch area. It is incorrect to say that such behaviour cannot be modified, although it is true that sniffing is so natural to all dogs that we have to provide a very strong incentive to achieve change. Remember, we must try to produce an alternative behaviour which is more beneficial to the dog. How do we go about this?

A. Sniffing at people

CURE

The dog that sniffs at crotches is fairly easily modified. Simply teach the dog to sit at your side as shown on the opposite page, and then ask your visitors to do the same. The dog will not be physically capable of sniffing this area when its bottom is on the ground at your side! Small dogs are rarely a problem as they cannot reach high enough.

OOOOOOOOOH!

B. Following a trail

CURE

The dog with its nose glued to the ground offers a greater problem. You can modify its behaviour by teaching a variety of different exercises.

1. First of all teach your dog to come when called (Exercise 1) so that it responds with alacrity every time you call, whether it is on a trail or not.
2. Teach your dog to heel beside you off the lead (Exercise 4), reinforcing it for *looking up at you*. Train when your dog is really eager for food and to start with use an area with no exciting smells.
3. You can also encourage your dog to hold its head up by teaching it to retrieve (Exercise 5). A retrieving dog has to carry its head high so that the article clears the ground.

NOTE: Don't think that the act of reinforcing your dog to keep its head up while it walks beside you or calling it away from a trail will spoil its ability to track if you are interested in this activity. Sniffing is such a strong innate behaviour that your dog will soon learn that the tracking harness is an opportunity to use its nose as nature intended.

THE *Sit at Side* EXERCISE

▮NITIAL CONDITIONING

1. As your dog approaches you, turn your body so that the dog comes to your left-hand side and then bring your right hand, containing food, to a position in front of the dog's nose.

2. Raise your hand upwards in a flowing motion to approximately waist level *directly* above the dog's head.

3. Say 'sit', as soon as the dog starts to adopt the sit position.

4. Reinforce the dog immediately its bottom touches the ground.

5. Remove your hand quickly up to waist level.

6. Repeat points 1–5 until the dog's behaviour becomes predictable.

Maintain conditioning by eliminating food in your hand as a stimulus and reinforcing your dog intermittently with food from your pocket.

PROBLEM 6 'GARBAGE GUTS' OR 'FUSSY FIDO'

When we discussed the dog's ingestive behaviour in Chapter 5, we commented on the fact that dogs are opportunistic feeders and will eat almost anything that comes their way. Our dogs' food-related problems are most often due to their natural desire to eat whenever they can, but an increasing number of pets are beginning to do the opposite: in other words to become picky or finicky eaters. This is definitely abnormal.

Other problems are associated with the dogs' natural instinct to chase and hunt for food. They have a tendency to eat harmoniously at a carcass but often become possessive of a bone or chunk of meat which they can tear off the carcass, take away, and regard as their own.

A. Stealing

CAUSE
● What we regard as stealing from the kitchen bench, barbeque or dining table is frankly not stealing to the dog! Dogs are not concerned with morality! Thieving is simply the act of eating what you can, when you can, in order to survive.

PREVENTION
Never leave food around where your dog can reach it. There is no point in leaving temptation staring them in the face!

CURE
It is not possible to suppress a dog's inborn drive to eat in order to survive, nor would we want to. However, it is relatively easy to condition a dog not to eat from certain places like the dining table or kitchen bench, places where we often leave food lying around. You can do this by teaching a fairly simple 'food refusal' exercise which gives your dog the desire to limit its eating to more appropriate places! It is a good way of teaching manners at mealtimes too. The exercise is taught at floor level first of all. When the dog has learnt to leave the food on the floor alone, it is then easy to teach it to leave food alone in other positions and situations.

THE THIEF!

THE *Food Refusal* EXERCISE

1. Sit or stand your dog at your left-hand side, (Exercise 2). Say 'wait' while offering the usual stay hand signal, see end of Exercise 3.

   NOTE: The word 'wait' is substituted for 'stay' because you are eventually going to signal your dog to break from the stay position.

2. Holding a piece of fresh meat in your right hand, place an *empty* bowl in front of your dog with your left hand. Say 'leave' and immediately reinforce the dog with food from your hand. If the dog looks at the dish make a gesture with your right hand to encourage it to look up at you. Feed the dog immediately.

3. Repeat points 1 and 2 a number of times with the empty dish.

4. Now place some 'boring' food such as diced carrots in the dish. Repeat points 1 and 2, making sure that your dog knows that you are carrying the more desirable food, i.e. meat. Gradually extend the time between putting the dish on the ground and offering the reinforcement.

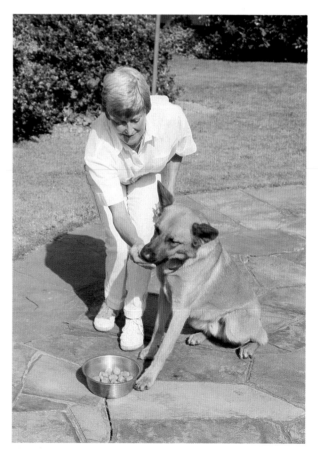

5. Next place meat, bones and your dog's dinner in the dish. Be alert for the slightest movement from your dog which would indicate an interest in the food in the dish. Repeat points 1 and 2, starting by reinforcing the dog immediately after you have said 'leave', then heeling it away from the dish by giving a big signal with meat in your hand. Gradually extend the time until the dog will sit and wait for a longer period, say 15 to 30 seconds, before reinforcing it. You have now reached the point where your dog can be reinforced by allowing it to eat the food in the dish. You can practise this exercise before each mealtime if you wish. Wait for varying lengths of time each day before pointing to the dish and saying 'yours', 'eat' or whatever word you favour.

NOTE: Never say 'leave' in a threatening way, or punish the dog for making a move towards the bowl. This can cause bizarre reactions such as fear of you, or avoiding the bowl. Simply go back to the start of the teaching procedure and gradually progress to the stage you wish to reach.

6. Now that your dog has learnt that leaving food alone on signal is advantageous to it, you can set up a situation where food is left hanging over the edge of the kitchen bench in an obvious manner! Use the same teaching procedure as before, saying 'leave' and reinforcing your dog with food from your hand.

7. Repetition of this exercise will quickly condition your dog to leave food on the kitchen bench alone. You can repeat the whole thing in any area where food is frequently left unattended.

An added advantage to teaching this exercise is that you will be able to signal your dog to 'leave' potentially dangerous substances such as chicken and chop bones which are frequently left on the ground in picnic areas. It can also be signalled to 'leave' cats, birds or aggressive looking dogs!

B. Raiding dustbins

CAUSE

⬤ This is another form of 'stealing' which dogs do not recognise as such! Dogs don't know about rubbish; they only know about finishing up anything that is edible. Often the smellier it is, the better! Dogs frequently eat carrion in the wild.

THE RAIDER!

PREVENTION

Purchase for yourself dog proof bins which have a hinged lid which cannot be knocked off. Don't allow your dog to go close to bins in the street or the park except when you are near enough to supervise them.

CURE

The problem of raiding dustbins can be dealt with in the same way as stealing from the kitchen bench, by teaching the dog to 'leave' the dustbin and reinforcing it for doing so. Initially you can set up a situation where the bin is full of material which is unpleasant to the dog so that it is less motivated to want to take anything from it. Look at it from the dog's point of view. The bin smells horrid whereas you are offering the ultimate benefit, its favourite food. What would you choose to do under the circumstances?

Obviously this will only work if your dog is monitored constantly while you are modifying the 'raiding bins' behaviour. One reinforcement in the form of a bin full of yummy scraps will induce the dog to raid bins at every opportunity! The name of the game is prevention, prevention, prevention.

C. Competing for food

CAUSE

⬤ ⬤ In the wild, wolves or feral dogs eat from the entire carcass of an animal in a large group, but once an individual tears off a chunk of meat or a bone it seems to own it. This is rather like people at a smorgasbord. We know that the contents of the table is for us all, but we regard the food on our plate as ours. Dogs usually move away from the group so that they can eat their bone or chunk of meat without competition. Possession seems to be nine-tenths of the law and even superior dogs will rarely try to take food from an inferior. Dogs usually obey this unwritten canine law and do not attempt to take food from other dogs. If they do try, one snap from the possessor of the food is usually enough to make the other dog back off.

Dogs will often share a bowl of soft food or drink from the same dish, just as they would share a carcass or a drink from the river. It is not usual for them to possess or defend these types of foodstuffs.

However, a problem can arise when one dog starts to subtly intimidate another dog. It usually happens like this: two dogs are given food in two separate bowls. One finishes more quickly than the other and

---

then starts to stare the other one down. Often the slower dog will give up eating and move away. The other dog then moves in and is reinforced for his actions by eating the other dog's food. The slow eater may develop a nutritional deficiency while the fast eater becomes more and more likely to refine his pressure tactics! The situation can become serious if the dogs are not supervised while eating and, as is frequently the case, the owner does not realise what is going on. Many people just assume that the slow dog has had enough to eat and that is why it moves away.

PREVENTION AND CURE

The solution is probably the easiest to implement of all the problems in this book. You can either feed the dogs in separate areas or give the slower dog its meal before the faster one. Alternatively, the latter can be called away from the eating area as soon as it has finished its own meal. In this case, you should intermittently reinforce the dog for coming to you with a little of its dinner which you have kept back for this purpose.

D. *Guarding food from people*

CAUSE

● ● Occasionally a dog will snap at, or bite, a human who comes too close to its food bowl or bone while it is feeding, particularly if the person is not one of its family group. We have mentioned before that this is normal dog behaviour, but in our society it could result in a death sentence even if the dog had a good reason for doing it! So it is most important that we teach our dogs to recognise that people around the food bowl are good news.

GIVING UP A BONE

PREVENTION

Ideally, we should begin this process when we first bring a puppy home. Hand feeding the pup with food from a dish will quickly make it realise that humans are associated with wonderful things around the food bowl. Friends, and small children, should also be asked to do this.

A couple of variations on the same theme will bring about a similar result. Place some dry food in a dish. While the pup is eating, frequently go up to the dish

Investigatory   Ingestive   Eliminative   Care Seeking   Shelter Seeking   Agonistic

and *add* something really tasty like chicken, cheese or fresh meat. The pup will welcome each visit! Also try giving the pup a raw flat bone to chew. After a few minutes go up to it and offer it a chunk of tasty meat. As the pup drops the bone to take the piece of food, say 'give' and take the bone away. Be careful never to lunge forward towards the pup to take the bone as this may develop an avoidance reaction. When the pup has finished the meat give it back the bone. Again the pup will become conditioned to the fact that giving up a bone is beneficial and, after a few repetitions, you can start taking the bone away and only offering an occasional reinforcement. Children should also be asked to go through these processes while the pup is small.

CURE

But . . . you may ask, what about the adult dog who has already got into an established habit of snapping or biting? In this case, you must start by changing the environment in which the dog is fed so that it is less likely to be triggered into an act of aggression. We suggest that you take the dog outside and scatter some dry food over 2 to 3 square metres of the garden.

While it is moving around eating this, approach the area and offer one or two pieces of its favourite food from your hand at ground level. Repeat this *every time the dog is fed* until it appears to be welcoming your approach. Gradually reduce the area where you scatter the dry food until it is piled up as it would be in its bowl, but continue to go up and offer tasty pieces of food by hand while it is eating the dry food. Progress to putting the dry food in a bowl, but still place it outside in the garden and repeat the same procedure. Then move to a neutral area inside the house, doing the same thing, and finally to the dog's former eating spot. Members of the family and confident friends can all be involved in offering the treats, so that all humans become synonymous with the reinforcement offered by the dog's favourite food.

Continue to do this intermittently to maintain your dog's response. At other times you can give the dog its normal meal, including fresh meat, tinned food, etc.

NOTE: For obvious reasons you should never involve children in the retraining of a dog that snaps or bites.

E. Dogs with picky eating habits

CAUSE

+ In our practice we are now seeing an increasing number of dogs who are indifferent towards food, eating only what they choose to eat and often ignoring the more nutritious parts of their diet. This is definitely **not** a normal dog behaviour!

Breeders are sometimes guilty of advising new owners to feed their pups too frequently. We have heard of owners being advised to feed their eight week old pup six times a day! Of course the breeders do this with the best of intentions; they want the pups to grow up strong and healthy. Inadvertently, they can cause a lot of problems!

When a litter of pups is fed from one dish they tend to eat normally because they are in competition with each other. Eat now, or get none, is the name of the game and so they learn to 'wolf' their food down. Then the pup goes to its new home. It is fed frequently and it is fed alone without any other pup competing. It is bulging with food! And more is on the way! It starts to leave some food and the owner offers something different to tempt it. He or she begins to leave food lying around in case the pup gets hungry.

A sure recipe for disaster! Fairly quickly, a pup can be changed from an avaricious eater to a picky indifferent eater who only likes chicken or prime steak!

The same thing can happen to an older dog if it goes to a new home or is fed by a different person. We have found the following feeding regime very successful in modifying a dog's abnormal attitude to food.

CURE:
A FEEDING REGIME

NOTE: This regime is suitable only for **healthy** dogs and pups. It is not designed for dogs who have been put on a special diet for a disease such as diabetes or a kidney disorder. Nor should it be used for a dog which is not eating because it is unwell — in these cases, please consult your veterinarian.

1. Feed an eight week old puppy a maximum of three meals a day. Cut this down to two meals as soon as the pup shows any disinterest in food, or at twelve weeks of age at the latest. From sixteen weeks of age onwards, give one meal only, at a time to suit yourself, unless the dog is obviously

underweight. As a rough guide its ribs should not be showing but you should be able to feel them under the skin.

2. Leave food in a bowl on the floor for five to ten minutes at the most. If there is any food remaining after this time, remove it and do not offer anything until the next scheduled meal. Make the next meal smaller until the dog is eating everything that is offered.

3. Never be tempted to offer alternative food if your dog does not eat what is put in front of it. Believe us, in the vast majority of cases the dog will not deprive itself of food for more than two to three days. It will usually start to eat like a normal dog after that time provided you do not weaken! It will be much fitter and healthier as a result, and you will always be able to tell if your dog is unwell. If a dog with a normal healthy appetite stops eating, it is a sure sign that something is wrong.

4. Fresh water should be available at all times unless your veterinarian advises otherwise for a particular reason, such as a tendency to bloat.

In 99 per cent of cases, fussy eating habits will be cured by following the regime just discussed. However, we have met a handful of dogs who were genuinely difficult to motivate to eat. In our experience Siberian Huskies are most prone to this problem, probably because they have been bred to travel long distances on a small intake of food, and we have also seen German Shepherds who are totally disinterested in food. One German Shepherd lost interest in food after it had been in a shelter for some time, while another would not eat for ten days after coming home following an operation. This is how David went about curing these dogs . . .

He advised the owners to leave a trail of food along a track in the park, then go back and collect the dog who was allowed to 'discover' the food and eat it as they walked. In each case, the dog seemed to be motivated by this natural hunting action and started to eat more normally. The same process was repeated until the dog was searching keenly and eating greedily. Once the pattern was set the owners could progress to feeding at home from a bowl every twenty-four or thirty-six hours. It is particularly important that owners of these types of dogs do not attempt to feed their dogs too frequently as this is definitely counterproductive.

NOTE: We were consulted about a dog which was being force fed because it would not eat. We had heard that acupuncture could help such cases and advised the owner accordingly. The dog was cured in two sessions by a veterinarian with experience in acupuncture.

WHAT KIND OF FOOD SHOULD WE FEED OUR DOG?

It is not the purpose of this book to advise on what you should feed your dog in any great detail, as there are a number of good books on dog nutrition written by knowledgeable authors. However, you may find some general nutritional principles useful.

Dogs, as we have learnt, enjoy most types of food, although we do know of a few who refuse fresh meat. Probably this is because fresh meat was not offered to them when they were young. It can also happen if a dog is not allowed to eat red meat for a period of time after a bout of gastroenteritis.

We recommend that you offer a variety of foods such as fresh meat, dry food, pureed vegetables, unsweetened cereals, filleted fish, rice, eggs, yoghurt, cheese and tinned dog food. Occasionally a raw marrow or brisket bone should be given after a meal rather than before, so that there is some roughage in the bowel to help the pieces of bone pass through. Bones should constitute part of the meal rather than be an addition to it, otherwise you may end up with an overweight animal!

We believe that some chunks of meat and dry food should be given daily with other food. This satisfies the dog's need to chew, exercises its jaws and gut and helps to clean its teeth. Canned food is nutritionally well balanced, but it does not satisfy the latter criteria so it should not constitute the whole meal. Nutritional supplements are not required if the dog is given some dry food each day, as dry food has minerals and vitamins added to it. Owners can inadvertently cause problems for their dog by over supplementation.

Milk can be difficult for some dogs to digest, as they lose the ability to break down the milk sugar (lactose) once they have been weaned. This can result in diarrhoea or loose stools. Soy milk is a good alternative as it does not contain lactose, or you can simply stop giving milk altogether.

Spoiled or spicy food should never be given to dogs.

Investigatory   Ingestive   Eliminative   Care Seeking   Shelter Seeking   Agonistic

F. Storing surplus food

The problem of storing surplus food by digging holes and burying it is dealt with in Problem 15.

G. Killing domestic livestock

This is a problem related to hunting behaviour rather than a food-related problem and is dealt with in Problem 13A.

PROBLEM 7 PROBLEMS WITH THE PLUMBING

The first step we must take when dealing with problems of elimination is to decide whether the cause is physical or behavioural. As a general rule, if the problem starts suddenly in an adult dog it is more likely to be physical in origin. Urinary tract infections, cancer, hormonal imbalance, neurological damage, operative procedures and degenerative changes associated with ageing can all affect your dog's bladder control. Such things as bacterial or viral infections of the gastro-intestinal tract or food poisoning can cause diarrhoea. The solution to these problems involves consulting your veterinarian who will determine the cause and treat it accordingly.

The only problem of this kind which will be discussed here concerns the young puppy or adult dog who is not yet house trained. It is usually the first problem that owners encounter when they bring a young pup home.

A. *House training a puppy*

Often the first question we are asked when clients bring a young puppy for training is 'What is the secret of successful house training?' They have tried smacking the pup when it wets in the house, rubbing its nose in its droppings, giving it a dirt box and putting paper down on the laundry floor — all to no avail. There are no magic remedies, but there *is* a simple and effective teaching process which will bring about speedy results.

The need to urinate or defecate is as natural a function for dogs as it is for humans. It takes a long time to toilet train a baby, yet puppies are expected to know what to do almost instantly! At eight weeks old a puppy has little bladder or bowel control, but it will develop them rapidly over the next couple of months. To teach or condition a puppy to eliminate in a certain spot we need to know two things, that is, the natural eliminative behaviour of wolves and dogs (Chapter 5: Eliminative behaviour) and how puppies learn (Chapter 7).

Remember that, if we reinforce or reward a response such as urinating outside with something which is important to the puppy such as a piece of food, then the puppy will tend to respond by urinating outside again when it is stimulated by a full bladder.

House training should start the moment you arrive home with your puppy so that you avoid having any 'accidents' right from the beginning. We suggest that you start before you even enter the house by taking the puppy to the area you want it to use. Let it explore the area and, if it obliges by urinating or defecating, praise it and give it a small piece of food. Incidentally the spot that you choose for the toilet area should not be too far from the house as you won't want to walk too far on cold wet nights!

Now take your pup inside and follow these instructions:

1. Set your watch or alarm clock to ring in one hour. When this time is up, walk your puppy outside to 'the spot' and stay there for five minutes or so. If it urinates or defecates, praise it and give it a small piece of food, then take it inside and set your alarm for another hour, and so on. If your puppy does not oblige during the five minute period, take it inside but go out ten minutes later and keep doing this until your patience is rewarded. You will quickly work out your little puppy's own rhythm.
2. Also, take the puppy out as soon as it wakens from sleep, after eating or drinking and when it has been chewing on a toy or after prolonged play.
3. Watch its body language carefully for any signs which may indicate a need to go out. Circling and sniffing are often signs it wants to go to the toilet.
4. When you are not able to watch your puppy for a while, either leave it in a secure part of the garden or confine it to a small area in the house such as

Investigatory | Ingestive | Eliminative | Care Seeking | Shelter Seeking | Agonistic

a baby's playpen. The playpen should contain the puppy's bed and a non-spill bowl of water. A playpen has the distinct advantage of being portable so you can move it from room to room and keep half an eye on the puppy. You will recall that a pup has a natural tendency not to soil its sleeping area, so it will tend to move around or whine in the playpen when it wants to go out, which should give you ample opportunity to walk it outside to your selected toilet area.

You have probably gathered by now that what you are doing is anticipating the puppy's behaviour (elimination) so that you can produce the response you want (the pup eliminating in the garden) which in turn is reinforcing or beneficial to the puppy, especially if you offer a piece of food straight after the act.

Obviously your ability to house train your puppy will be much better if you are able to supervise it regularly for the first two to three weeks. Try to arrange holidays if possible – see Chapter 2: Prepare for your puppy's homecoming.

NIGHT TIME HOUSE TRAINING

A pup's bladder is not mature enough to go through the night without emptying. You can deal with this by taking your pup out just before you go to bed and then confining it to the playpen which you can place close to your bed. Attach a small bell to your pup's collar so that the tinkle wakens you when the puppy becomes restless. If you are a heavy sleeper you will need to set your alarm and take the puppy out a maximum of five to six hours after you went to bed. Protect your carpet in case of accidents!

There are some people who prefer to leave their pup outside or in the laundry at night. We don't recommend that you do either, as both will make the pup stressed by being alone. Remember that you have taken it away from its litter so it is your responsibility to give the puppy your companionship instead.

Leaving the puppy in the laundry is also counterproductive to your house training programme as the pup will be forced to urinate in the house. Whether you put paper down on the floor is immaterial; you have still caused the pup to wet in the house. If you are prepared to get up once or twice during the night to take the pup out, this will help, but it will not solve the stress of social isolation.

ACCIDENTS IN THE HOUSE

Inevitably one or two accidents will happen, nobody is perfect! It is extremely important never to punish your puppy for eliminating in the house because the pup will associate the punishment with 'the act' rather than its location. In other words, it will be frightened to urinate or defecate in front of you and will try to hide next time it needs to eliminate. This will be most distressing for the puppy and will cause *major* house training problems.

When accidents happen you should clean the area thoroughly and then deodorise it so that there is no smell of urine left, otherwise the puppy will tend to go back and use that spot again. Don't use ammonia-based cleaning products which will smell like urine to the dog!

The cardinal rules of house training are patience, observation, and the application of appropriate knowledge so that you can produce, and reinforce, the behaviour you want.

REMEMBER

1. Take your puppy out frequently while it is awake, and immediately after eating or sleeping.
2. Let it walk to the door to establish the pattern of going to the door when it needs to go out.
3. Reinforce your puppy with praise and a piece of food when it urinates or defecates outside.
4. Never punish your puppy if it makes a 'mistake'. Clean the area thoroughly and be more observant next time!

If you follow this advice, your puppy should be house trained within two weeks. A marvellous feat considering it may take a human years!

NOTE: Once your puppy is house trained, you can teach it to use a doggy door (Problem 18) so that it can get out to eliminate whenever it needs to.

B. *House training an adult dog*

Adult dogs who are not house trained have usually not had the opportunity to learn that urinating and defecating inside a house is taboo. Generally speaking, they have been raised in a kennel or some other restricted area and have not been taken out regularly enough to establish a pattern of eliminating outside their 'enclosure'. It can be surprisingly difficult to get the message across to these dogs as they have built up a strong habit of urinating and defecating wherever, and whenever, the need arises. And, of course, elimination, because it gives relief, is reinforcing in its own right like hunting or chasing.

For an adult dog you should follow the suggestions we have given for house training puppies. Don't fall into the trap of expecting it to learn faster because it is adult and you think it should 'know better' or should be able to 'hang on'. Patience, perseverance and reinforcement will triumph in the end!

Incidentally, the urine of bitches can have a disastrous effect on your lawn and on some plants. You can overcome this by taking her to a particular spot and reinforcing her for urinating there. Our Golden Retriever bitch uses the ivy if necessary. It seems unusually hardy! If your bitch does urinate on the lawn, water the area thoroughly as soon as possible afterwards.

Many dogs of both sexes like to wait until they leave the garden if they have the opportunity, as they prefer to eliminate where other dogs have been before. After all, this is natural behaviour in the wild.

C. *Wetting from fright*

CAUSE

● ● A dog which lies on its side with one leg elevated and urinates is displaying the ultimate submissive gesture to defuse potential aggression in another dog.

● ● Fear-induced urination most commonly occurs when dogs are harshly treated. It can become a habit which a dog will display in anticipation of punishment. A dog may also defecate and empty its anal glands in fear. This is a physiological reaction common to many species. Some breeds are more sensitive than others and are more likely to exhibit this type of behaviour.

PREVENTION AND CURE

Dogs should never be put in a situation where they eliminate in fear of people. If this does happen, human reactions such as shouting, threatening or punishing are absolutely taboo and indeed probably caused the behaviour in the first place. The problem can, and will, be modified quickly if everyone who comes into contact with the dog follows these rules:

1. Never punish the dog under any circumstances.
2. Avoid patting the dog when it is in a submissive position.
3. Teach the 'recall' (Exercise 1), reinforcing the dog frequently until it associates coming to you with the benefit of food. Be particularly careful not to reinforce any kind of avoidance behaviour such as the dog stepping away from you or cringing.
4. Ask your family and friends to do the same so that the dog realises that all humans are 'good news'.
5. Expose the dog to all sorts of different environments and to other dogs, making every interaction a good experience. This socialisation will increase boldness.

NOTE: If your dog is extremely fearful your progress may be very slow and you will have to follow the advice on fear-related behaviour laid down in Problem 10A.

D. *Wetting in excitement*

CAUSE

● Young pups are less able to control their bladders than older dogs.

✛ Puppies are often subjected to fairly long periods of social isolation and may become excessively excited when the owner comes home or visitors arrive.

PREVENTION AND CURE

As the problem nearly always occurs when a pup jumps up on someone's legs, the solution involves anticipating and preventing this particular behaviour.

| Investigatory | Ingestive | Eliminative | Care Seeking | Shelter Seeking | Agonistic |

1. Arm yourself with some pieces of food which you have prepared in readiness for your return home.

2. As the pup rushes up to you, drop your right hand containing food down to the pup's nose level and reinforce it in the stand position.

3. Move back rapidly and repeat point 2 a number of times, taking care never to offer food if the dog is urinating.

4. Once the initial excitement has died down, you can produce other responses such as the 'sit' (Exercise 2) and 'sit stay' (Exercise 3), so that the pup is reinforced for passive responses.

It will also help if you:

1. Try to avoid long periods of isolation for the puppy by arranging for a friend or neighbour to visit it if you have to be away from home for a few hours.

2. Walk the pup at least twice a day. This will help to calm it down, keep it exercised and content and, most importantly, the pup will learn about the world outside the back garden.

3. Avoid patting the pup when it is excited as this will only increase its activity. Stroke it when it is lying down quietly after exercise.

4. Finally, never punish the pup if it does urinate in excitement. Simply try to prevent this from happening next time. In all probability the situation will improve spontaneously as the pup matures.

E. Too many calling cards

Male dogs occasionally lift their legs and urinate on places which are not socially acceptable such as on trouser legs, in a strange house or on top of toys which have been left lying in the garden.

CAUSE

● Male dogs start to lift their legs and deposit urine on elevated objects from puberty onwards. 'Marking' has great social and sexual significance to dogs.

● A dog that goes into a strange house and urinates there usually does so because there is an odour which stimulates him to act in that way. Perhaps another dog urinated there in the past and the area was either not cleaned properly or cleaned with an ammonia-based product which smells like urine to a canine nose!

PREVENTION AND CURE

1. Always clean any area which has been sprayed with urine thoroughly with vinegar and water and then apply a deodorant.

2. Entire dogs do mark more frequently than castrated males and, if all else fails, castration may be worth considering if this has not already been done. Apparently it helps in some cases.

3. We have seen a number of dogs cock their legs on people who have been standing in the park! Presumably their leg just looked like any other elevated object or tree trunk! Perhaps the person had brushed against urine soaked grass or they had patted another dog along the way. Keep moving . . .!

4. In the same way, children's toys just look like any other interesting object to pee on. Remove them from sight when they are not being used.

F. A distasteful habit: eating faeces

We have not encountered many dogs who eat faeces. Not dogs' faeces that is! Eating the stools of herbivorous animals is absolutely normal for dogs and does them no harm in moderation. In fact, they are a useful source of nutrients for wolves or feral dogs when other food is in short supply. However, eating their own faeces or the faeces of other dogs is a different matter and should be discouraged because it can spread parasites such as roundworm and whipworm.

CAUSE

+ + Some people think that this habit is due to a nutritional deficiency but personally we feel it is more likely to be caused by boredom (Problem 1). The habit can develop in young pups who are confined to a small area with little to amuse them. Dogs who have a reasonable amount of freedom rarely develop the problem.

PREVENTION AND CURE

Whatever the reason, the solution seems obvious. Simply take your dog out at least twice a day, particularly after eating, so that it can defecate away from home. Remember to clean up after it. Call it away from any droppings you come across on your walk and reinforce it with a piece of meat for coming to you. This should quickly persuade your dog that there are better things to eat than stools. Also do the rounds of the garden at least once a day and dispose of any faeces.

Try giving your dog a large raw bone to chew, two or three times a week, which it may prefer to eating faeces.

Some people have experimented with additives in the diet which give the stools a disagreeable odour and taste with varying results. Make sure your dog's diet is well balanced just in case it does have a deficiency.

NOTE: Bitches who clean up after they have stimulated their pups to urinate and defecate should not be discouraged from eating the deposits. This is a natural behaviour designed to keep the den or bed clean.

THE FLOW OF LIFE

PROBLEM 8 **P**UPPIES THAT MOUTH AND BITE

The problem of puppies mouthing and biting is on a par with house training as the number one concern of new puppy owners. Is it normal behaviour? Yes. Can it cause problems? Decidedly yes!

CAUSE

● Mouthing is a normal exploratory behaviour in all pups. They investigate everything that they can reach with their mouths just like human babies. Not everyone takes into consideration the fact that pups are at a distinct disadvantage because they walk on all fours and do not have hands with which to hold and manipulate things.

PLAY MOUTHING

● Teething is a painful process and most young creatures seem to need to bite and chew to relieve the pain in their gums. Puppies are teething almost constantly from about three weeks to five or six months of age!

● It is natural for pups to possess objects by picking them up and storing them, e.g. bones, but in the domestic environment shoes, socks and pieces of wood are all fair game.

● Human play activities often promote mouthing, e.g. if a child runs with the puppy this can lead to an instinctive chase and hunt response. Part of hunting is biting your prey!

Investigatory   Ingestive   Eliminative   Care Seeking   Shelter Seeking   Agonistic

MY UNDOING

● Loose trousers, long flowing skirts, shoe laces and leads may all trigger off the chase and bite instinct. Even a movement such as sitting cross-legged and waving one foot in front of the pup is an exciting stimulus, particularly for herding breeds which are very tuned into rounding up anything that moves.

✛ Humans who tease pups either inadvertently or deliberately may cause pain, annoyance and increased aggression in any age of dog. Common actions such as flicking a towel at the pup, boxing it around the face, pushing it away, patting it roughly on the rump or grabbing its tail may all seem like good fun but can lead to **enormous problems**.

PREVENTION AND CURE

Having identified why the behaviour develops, the preventive strategies and solutions become almost self-evident.

1. Provide chew toys such as rawhide, uncooked brisket bone and the occasional marrow bone. Put shoes, pot plants and other items out of reach.
2. Avoid wearing loose flapping clothing or shoes while the pup is young. If this is impractical, distract the pup from your clothes by rolling a ball or tossing one of its toys along the ground. Make the alternative more exciting than your movements.
3. Teach children to be passive around the puppy as discussed under Problem 23B.
4. *Never* tease pups or play with them roughly. In particular, do not play tug of war with excitable dogs or breeds such as terriers with a genetically programmed tendency to hold onto things.
5. Teach the puppy to heel beside you off lead (Exercise 4). Then introduce a long light lead, giving the pup exactly the same hand and voice signals as for the heel off lead. It will already be conditioned to walk beside you in a controlled manner. This will stop it from getting into the habit of biting the lead.
6. Pat the puppy when it is quiet after exercise rather than in the excitement of a home coming.
7. Teach exercises such as the 'sit stay' (Exercise 3) so that you reinforce passive responses.
8. Puppies quickly learn to control their bite when they are playing with their litter mates. The high-pitched yelp of a sibling when play becomes too rough seems to make the biter back off immediately. You should mimic this sound if your pup nips you.

   Punishing your pup for biting will only increase the aggression of a bold puppy and make a fearful pup even more timid. Just think how you react to physical pain!
9. Some puppies and dogs who have never been given food by hand seem to have some trouble discriminating between fingers and food! The easiest way to change this is to present a clenched fist to the dog's mouth and then unfold your fingers to reveal the food.

PROBLEM *9* **C**AR SICKNESS

CAUSE

+ Many puppies and older dogs suffer from nausea and vomiting when they first travel in a car. Initially, the symptoms are probably due to the irregular motion which disturbs the organ of balance in the inner ear. Also, the anxiety caused by being taken away from litter mates and put in a strange moving environment may make the puppy's first experience of the car more likely to induce nausea. Thereafter the car may become associated with frightening consequences. A vicious circle is established with anxiety leading to vomiting, and vomiting leading to increased anxiety.

MEALS ON WHEELS

PREVENTION AND CURE

It may be worth considering giving a puppy or inexperienced dog a mild sedative half an hour before departure to help it cope with the journey to its new home, especially if this is going to involve hours of travel. Ask your veterinarian about appropriate medication and dose.

However, we are not advising you to give medication on a regular basis. You will quickly encourage your puppy or dog to enjoy car travel if you go about it in the following way:

1. Take your dog's meal outside and place it in the car while your dog watches you. Allow the dog to jump in and eat it. The act of jumping into the car will be instantly reinforced. Repeat this a number of times while the car is stationary.

Investigatory   Ingestive   Eliminative   Care Seeking   Shelter Seeking   Agonistic

2. Take your dog for short car rides which finish with a walk in the park or some other pleasurable experience. Start by driving a kilometre or so, and work up to longer distances depending on your dog's reaction.

3. You can feed the dog with small pieces of food while you are travelling provided it looks bold and happy.

Incidentally, we made a classic error with our Golden Retriever who was reluctant to go in the car. Her first journey involved travelling from an area just south of Sydney all the way to Melbourne. She was very sick and emptied her bowels.

A few short trips later, she started to salivate almost as soon as she got into the car. We offered her pieces of food as we travelled in an effort to persuade her that car travel was a happy event. This was a big mistake and we should have known better! All we achieved was to reinforce her salivation and anxiety. When we realised what we had done, we were able to modify her behaviour so that she jumped into the car with alacrity, but we certainly made the procedure more drawn out than it should have been. So make sure you only reinforce bold happy behaviour!

4. Avoid smoking in the car. This can make humans feel very nauseated, so we're sure it could also affect your dog.

5. Provide fresh air, either by opening vents or travelling with a window slightly open. Do not let your dog travel with its head out of the window as this can lead to eye damage.

6. On long journeys, stop frequently for a walk and fresh air. This will benefit you, too!

7. Position the dog in an area which is less likely to be subject to vibration. The back of a station wagon or a seat in the car is better than the floor.

8. On hot days, place a damp towel underneath your dog if you don't have air conditioning.

9. If you have a small dog, it often helps if you build up the seat with something like a mattress so that the dog can sit up and look out.

And remember . . . **never** leave your dog confined in the car on a warm or hot day. The temperatures in a stationary car can rise dramatically in a very short period. Dogs are killed in this way every year.

Without fear no creature on this earth would survive. Fear unconsciously influences behaviour, preventing actions which could be harmful.

When observing how puppies learn (Chapter 3), we noticed how limited their reactions were to their environment up to approximately two weeks of age. Scientific experiments have shown that puppies less than three weeks old who have been exposed to frightening experiences show no memory of these events in later life.

From approximately three weeks onwards, when their hearing has developed and they have the capacity to stand and move on all four legs, pups have the ability to wander further afield to explore. They begin to associate painful or unpleasant experiences with whatever caused them and naturally try to avoid them in future. In other words they start to develop fear responses.

Observations of their interactions can be summarised on a scale as follows:

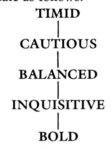

TIMID
|
CAUTIOUS
|
BALANCED
|
INQUISITIVE
|
BOLD

The temperament of older dogs will mirror these degrees, often combining some on each side of the point marked 'BALANCED', above. A **bold** dog will show some *caution* when investigating a new environment. Dogs that are referred to as 'fear biters' fall into the **timid** and **bold** class, i.e. they are dogs which are predominantly *timid* and who often find investigating new environments, people and dogs traumatic. They solve this by lunging forward in a bold manner in an effort to rid themselves of their problem and then quickly recoil back to their basic timid state. This imbalance is usually caused by inadequate socialisation and training (Chapter 2) or by being abnormally stressed when young. Their behaviour is hard to

predict and they may launch an attack without obvious provocation.

Between six and eight weeks of age puppies decide how they want to respond to their environment. If a puppy is startled by accidentally running into a puddle of water, then its next encounter with water will probably produce an avoidance response. Repetition of this event may make the puppy develop an aversion to water in general, whether it is from a hose or a tap, or in a dam or river.

Fear responses are easily developed, particularly during the critical socialisation period. Whilst genetic inheritance has a considerable influence on a dog's temperament, it is not the only factor which affects the total outcome. The various breeds of dog inherit a tendency to behave in certain ways, e.g. to herd sheep, but not all members of a breed are true to their inheritance. We've had many gun dogs and retrievers for training who will not look for, or bring back, anything!

Some pure bred dogs inherit a very sensitive disposition. The handsome Belgian Shepherd is one such breed. Incorrectly handled, this dog can exhibit flighty, nervous behaviour towards humans and other dogs. Breeders who specialise in breeds with a nervous tendency should select dogs and bitches for balanced temperament rather than primarily for their appearance.

Our dogs have to learn to cope with all the trappings of the domestic scene. The noise of washing machines, vacuum cleaners, lawn-mowers, guns, fireworks, chainsaws and cars can all create a great sense of anxiety and fear in the unconditioned puppy.

Dogs are frequently punished for eliminating in the 'wrong' spot, digging holes or howling all night, which only escalates their fear responses. Wolves, on the other hand, only have to cope with the noises that nature produces and there is no stress on them to conform to human expectations. Apart from the occasional bird noise or the howl of one of their pack, their world epitomises peace and tranquility. They have little to fear except when man arrives with his gun and traps.

A. Fear of humans

AVOIDANCE BEHAVIOUR

CAUSE

+ + By now it must be very clear that a pup which is deprived of meaningful socialisation during the early weeks of its life is likely to exhibit many of the fearful and aggressive responses that we observe in the adult dog.

PREVENTION

Prevention of these problems by early socialisation is obviously the best strategy (Chapter 2). However, you may already have an adult dog that is indicating that it is frightened of humans by hiding behind you or cringing away when another person comes near. The term 'avoidance behaviour' accurately describes this type of fear response. To overcome the problem, you need to generate non-avoidance or bold behaviour and then reinforce it. You can go about it in this way
. . . **Go through the process slowly.**

CURE

1. Make sure your dog is extremely keen to take food by delaying its normal mealtime for a number of hours.

2. Put the dog on a long light lead measuring approximately 3 metres.

3. Provide a friend with some pieces of your dog's favourite food. Ask her to walk slowly ahead of you holding her arms at her sides

with a piece of food in each hand. The food must be obvious to the dog.

NOTE: Dogs have nothing to fear if a person is walking away from them, the problem arises when someone approaches.

4. Allow your dog to catch up with your friend gradually and take the food. Your friend **must not stop** but should keep walking away slowly.

5. Your friend should replenish her hands with more pieces of food and allow your dog to repeat this action a number of times.

6. Repeat points 4 and 5, but this time your friend should pause for a few seconds when

the dog takes the food before moving off again. She must not turn and face the dog yet.

7. Repeat the previous action, except that your friend should modify her action slightly by pausing with her body partly turned towards

the dog. Repeat this procedure gradually reaching a point when your friend is facing the dog.

Consider the consequences of your actions so far.

(a) The dog has made only bold forward movements.

(b) Your friend did not promote any avoidance behaviour, simply because she moved away each time the dog approached.

(c) The dog made the decision to investigate, **not** to avoid.

(d) Your friend was seen as beneficial to the dog and not something to fear.

8. Repeat points 1–7 without the lead.

9. Next, your friend should call the dog from a distance of 1 to 2 metres. As it reaches her it must **immediately** be reinforced with food and your friend should step smoothly away from the dog, thereby leaving the dog in a bold state.

10. Repeat point 9, gradually getting your friend to call your dog from further and further away.

It is important that you, the handler, offer no benefit to the dog whatsoever during this process. The dog must learn to enjoy approaching everybody, not just its owner. So often we see nervous dogs being protected by their handlers by being kept on a short tight lead. These people actually promote and sustain their dog's bizarre behaviour. David often takes this type of dog for a short walk on a 3 metre lead. The moment

they are out of sight of the owner, the dog's attitude substantially improves. As he jokingly says to the owners: 'If we had you put down, your dog wouldn't have a problem!'

Up to this point, no physical contact has been made with the dog. Next comes the trickier stage, when your friend will start to touch the dog while both of you reinforce its response with food.

11. Both you and your friend should have food in your hand, making this obvious to the dog.

12. Ask your friend to take up a position a few paces away from you and your dog. Walk your dog up beside your friend and **immediately** give your dog a piece of food.

13. Your friend must then step away two or three paces without making any attempt to touch the dog.

14. Repeat points 12 and 13 several times.

15. Next walk your dog up beside your friend who should give the dog a piece of food while **you** touch your dog. Touch the dog on its chest or body rather than on its head.

16. Repeat point 15 but this time **your friend** should touch the dog at the **same time** as **you** offer the food. Repeat this numerous times.

17. Repeat point 16 but, instead of feeding your dog as your friend touches it, delay feeding momentarily so that the dog is reinforced *after* being touched.

18. Gradually increase the time between your friend touching the dog and offering the reinforcement.

19. Finally get to the stage where your friend can touch the dog while you maintain its behaviour by reinforcing it intermittently.

20. Repeat the whole procedure with numerous people, making sure that the dog is never stressed.

Offering food diminishes the impact of hand contact and makes the dog associate touch with great benefit.

Diagrammatically the process can be illustrated as follows:

FOOD WITHOUT   TOUCH

FOOD TOGETHER WITH TOUCH

TOUCH THEN FOOD

TOUCH THEN FOOD
INTERMITTENTLY

B. *Fear of other dogs*

Fear of other dogs can be as big a problem as chasing (Problem 13), because a panic-stricken dog may run under a car or get lost. Keeping your dog on the lead is counterproductive because the dog becomes even more dependent on you to protect it.

CAUSE

+ Lack of socialisation with other dogs, particularly during the critical socialisation period. The situation is exacerbated by well meaning veterinarians who advise their clients to keep their puppies isolated from other dogs until they have completed their immunisation regime, usually at sixteen weeks of age.

+ Some owners discourage contact with other dogs by keeping their own dog on a lead and pulling it away when it attempts to communicate with another animal.

+ Owners of small dogs are sometimes over protective and lift them up in their arms when another dog comes near.

● A traumatic experience with one dog, or a group of dogs, can result in either a generalised fear of all dogs, fear of the particular dog that caused the stress or of any animal which looks like the latter.

+ Some breeds have a propensity to be more watchful and are more likely to be triggered into an avoidance response, e.g. Shetland Sheepdogs. Compare this with the bold behaviour of terriers.

PREVENTION

1. Puppies must be socialised with other healthy, immunised puppies or quiet adult dogs on a regular basis, see Chapter 2: Socialise your puppy.
2. Be aware of the temperament potential of your breed of dog, taking particular care that a more nervous type of animal always has positive socialisation experiences.

CURE

1. Teach your dog to come when it is called so that you can control it when you go out walking (Exercise 1).

2. Arrange to meet a friend who has a placid friendly dog in a neutral area such as a park. Go for a walk together with the dogs off the lead. Keep moving rather than standing and chatting!

Feed the dogs together from individual bowls at the end of your walk. The previous meal should be delayed specifically for this purpose. Avoid creating a competitive situation over the food by feeding the dogs a few metres apart on the first occasion. Gradually bring the bowls closer together on subsequent meetings. This will make your dog regard the other dog as beneficial.

3. Once your dog is comfortable with one dog, you can then start to introduce it to other temperamentally sound animals, always walking together rather than standing still.

Owners of nervous dogs who attend us for temperament modification are sometimes encouraged to go to The Kintala Club, see page 14, and mix with instructors' dogs after training. They are advised to stay on the periphery of the group to start with so that the dogs meet individually rather than en masse. These dogs can usually quickly progress to walking with selected dogs.

Modifying fear behaviour involves a great deal of time and commitment on the part of the handler. Remarkable improvement can be made, but fearful dogs can rarely be 100 per cent cured.

C. Fear of loud noises

(cars backfiring, balloons bursting, guns firing, etc.)

CAUSE

● Dogs can become fearful of some sights or sounds because they are associated in their minds with an aversive event, e.g. someone we know had a dog that was hit by a car immediately after the car backfired. After that traumatic experience he became extremely agitated whenever he heard any similar sharp sound such as a balloon bursting or a cap gun going off. He literally shook uncontrollably.

● The unpredictable suddenness of a gunshot can induce dogs to run away in fright. A breeder of gun dogs, whose main interest was in gun dog trials, came to us for help. It appeared that a high percentage of litters that he had bred were gun-shy. When asked how he judged their tolerance level, he explained that he would take a litter of approximately eight puppies at about six months of age into a paddock and fire a round or two over their heads. Those that stayed close to him, he kept. Those that ran away were disposed of. On average only two survived to hear another gun shot! This totally inappropriate, insensitive and counterproductive method of assessment accounted for the disposal of many potentially excellent gun dogs.

CURE

The process of introducing a dog either to a real gun or cap gun is the same, but for ease of explanation we will use a cap gun and child scenario. It does not matter if you are conditioning a naive puppy or a mature dog, the procedure is the same. However, if the dog already has an established fear response to loud sharp noises, then you will have to progress more slowly.

1. Start the initial conditioning outside where the sound will dissipate and be less intense.

2. Ask a child to take up a position at least twenty paces away from you and your dog. Your dog should be keen for food and you should carry some pieces of your dog's favourite food.

3. On your signal, the child should fire the gun once only while you simultaneously give your dog one or two pieces of food.

4. Gradually decrease the distance between the child with the cap gun and the dog, reinforcing a bold response every time.

5. Repeat the entire procedure at varying distances and with the child and dog in different situations. Make your reinforcements intermittent.

6. Letting the dog eat its evening meal whilst the cap gun is fired at varying distances should be the next stage.

Do not give the dog any voice or hand signals whilst practising, as the absence of these signals when the dog is alone may trigger some feelings of insecurity. After all, the dog must learn to cope with loud noises whether you are there or not.

Obviously the explosive sound of a real gun is likely to startle a dog and affect its sensitive hearing. Imagine how you would react if someone suddenly picked up a gun and fired it over your head! At least you have an idea what to expect, whereas a dog does not.

A real gun should be first discharged at a minimum of 200 metres away from a naive or gun-shy dog and a similar conditioning procedure used. Obviously 'blanks' should be used and the person using the gun must fulfil any legal requirements such as having a gun licence.

Investigatory　Ingestive　Eliminative　Care Seeking　Shelter Seeking　Agonistic

D. *Fear of thunderstorms*

CAUSE

✦ Some dogs have a seemingly illogical fear of thunderstorms which in human terms might be classified as a phobia. Their reaction to the early rumblings is either to hide in a dark spot, usually under the house, or to frantically escape from the garden and run amuck. We knew one dog who would break down doors or scale very high fences in his panic. He came close to being shot on one occasion when he ran for a long distance and finished up in a paddock full of sheep. Fortunately the dog-ranger recognised him as a dog who regularly went missing during thunderstorms.

✦ There are some people who believe that dogs are more sensitive to storms because of the increased electricity in the air and the relatively high concentration of salt in a dog's blood. Salt increases electrical conduction in the body. However, the knowledge that we have of the dogs in our neighbourhood and at the club which David founded supports our theory that fear of thunder and lightning is conditioned, not inherited or innate. Comparatively few dogs seem to be aversely affected. Those that are can be treated by a process known as systematic desensitisation.

CURE

Obviously, you cannot wait until a thunderstorm develops in order to modify your dog's behaviour, but you can purchase a sound track with a realistic thunderstorm sequence such as that in Ferde Grofe's Grand Canyon Suite★ and start your desensitisation programme as follows:

1. Teach your dog to 'sit and stay' (Exercises 2 and 3) in the house and reinforce these responses with food.

2. Put the music on very low and repeat the sit and stay exercises, making sure that your dog is not stressed by the sound.

3. Gradually increase the volume, reinforcing the dog for remaining calm and relaxed. If it becomes agitated, do not reinforce it, but go back and begin again with a very low volume.

4. Progress to a point where you can go out and leave the tape on.

If possible try to be at home with your dog when the next real thunderstorm is forecast so that you can continue the desensitisation in the real life situation.

---

*Available on compact disc 1987 Telarc CD-80086.

PROBLEM *11* **T**HE EXCITABLE DOG

CAUSE

✚ ✚ Excitable behaviour is not common in the wild, where life is geared to survival. Wolves run together in the pursuit of prey or they use their energy to breed or raise young. Their most excitable responses occur when they greet each other. Humans have selectively bred dogs for various purposes and in so doing they have either deliberately or accidentally increased the excitability of some breeds such as Cocker Spaniels, Poodles and some of the herding breeds. Their excitable behaviour often takes the form of mad twirling, rushing, circling, constant barking or chasing anything that moves quickly, whether it constitutes a meal or not.

✚ Boredom and confinement can lead to bizarre stereotyped behaviour such as rushing up and down beside a barrier or leaping up and scrabbling at a fence.

✚ Young children can turn a normally placid puppy into a canine dervish if they chase it or play with it roughly!

PREVENTION

1. Choose a dog which is suited to your own activity level. An active excitable kind of dog may well be suitable for someone who likes to exercise, but would be totally inappropriate for a sedentary person.
2. Early socialisation of all dogs is very important if they are to grow up as well adjusted individuals (Chapter 2). Animals which are not exposed to different people, environments and other dogs may become abnormally excited by change.
3. Children should be taught to treat dogs properly and encouraged to be quiet and passive. Young children should be carefully monitored, while older children can be involved in the dog's training if they are interested (Problem 23B).

QUIET TIMES

Investigatory　　Ingestive　　Eliminative　　Care Seeking　　Shelter Seeking　　Agonistic

CURE

If your dog is already excitable there are other strategies which you can use:

1. Give the dog plenty of exercise off lead so that it can investigate and tire itself out. Teach it to come on signal first! (Exercise 1).
2. Eliminate any activities which trigger excitable behaviour, e.g. tug of war or taking your dog near motor bikes.
3. Actively reinforce passive responses such as teaching the dog the 'sit stay' (Exercise 3).
4. Try to remain quiet and calm yourself and give your dog a tranquil lifestyle.

CONTRASTS IN LIFE

Group　　　　Sexual　　　　Care Giving　　● Normal Behaviour　+ Modified Behaviour

PROBLEM *12* **A**GGRRRRRRESSION!

Social relationships between people are dependent upon innate or inborn behaviour and behaviour which is learnt in the company of others. It is not instinctive for humans to shake hands or kiss. Customs vary around the world. Some people greet one another by rubbing noses while others bow. Children are not comfortable with the act of shaking hands but, by continually observing adults reacting to friends or strangers, they learn that extending their hand and arm forward with a smile will usually promote an agreeable response. A person whose manner is aggravating or aggressive often stimulates a response that matches their mood.

Why should the social interactions of dogs be any different? They are not. Watching dogs is fascinating. They talk with their eyes, ears, head, body and tail movements (Chaper 6). Without verbal language what else can they do? Like human beings, the normal greeting behaviour between dogs is to meet cordially and then go their separate ways. But some dogs seem to be social misfits and don't care about the normal or acceptable thing to do. Fighting seems more beneficial to them, no matter how nice the other dog is.

Such dogs are incorrigible and have usually been raised or trained in an environment that promotes aggression. Dogs which are chained up for days, weeks or months on end forget their gentle puppy ways and learn to think that anything beyond the length of their chain is foreign or harmful and should be attacked. A similar reaction is produced if a dog is jerked in the neck by its owner every time it comes in contact with another dog. It learns to hate the presence of other dogs. Owners of these dogs often express verbal intolerance by growling the words 'leave it' at the same time. If the dog escapes or is allowed to go free, it is likely to perceive other dogs which it meets as a threat, and attack without warning or going through the normal social greeting behaviour. It has never had the opportunity to learn to behave appropriately; in fact the poor creature has been taught to behave inappropriately.

The human race seems to want to breed dogs with the aggressive tendencies evident in a number of breeds. The alert, bold and fearless nature of these dogs are characteristics that some breeders try to accentuate. When the natural animal, the wolf, can demonstrate to the world how to live in groups in harmony, friendliness and with an inhibition against fighting, why do we continue to exacerbate the errors of breeding which we have made in the past?

Terrier breeds find it difficult to live in groups. Puppies often have to be separated from one another as early as eight weeks of age. Their aggressive tendencies inhibit natural acts of socialisation. Ironically, one of the breeds that suffers a lot of malignment, the German Shepherd, develops with a minimum of hostility amongst the litter. If they are raised and trained without force, this breed will exhibit most of the qualities we desire in a dog. The same can be said of the more placid types of dog such as gun dogs and retrievers.

A. The aggro dog

AGGRESSION TOWARDS OTHER DOGS

CAUSE

+ Dogs are often restricted by leads, chains or fences so they are unable to investigate each other naturally.
+ Dogs are often deprived of the opportunity to socialise with other dogs, especially during the critical socialisation period, so they do not learn to communicate properly.

| Investigatory | Ingestive | Eliminative | Care Seeking | Shelter Seeking | Agonistic |

+ Rough behaviour such as punishing or threatening a dog may lead to increased canine aggression, particularly in 'superior' animals.

+ Owners who use sticks to prevent other dogs from coming close to their own are a frequent cause of aggression, both in their own dog and in the dog who bears the brunt of the stick.

+ Some breeds have been selectively bred for increased aggression, e.g. terriers. Some individuals within a breed may be more aggressive than others and may pass this tendency on to their offspring.

PREVENTION

The most frequent term used throughout this book is 'socialisation'. The implications of this word are many but, in the context of this problem, socialisation equals prevention.

By correctly socialising your dog from puppy to adulthood (Chapter 2), the likelihood of this problem occurring is negligible. However, some dog owners have not been told about the importance of socialisation and consequently they sometimes produce aggressive dogs. It is very difficult to completely modify the behaviour of a dog which is habitually aggressive towards other dogs, but there are some things you can do to help to control the situation.

CONTROL TECHNIQUES

1. Use a long lead (5 metres) when walking your dog.
2. Train your dog to 'come' to you using food as a reinforcement (Exercise 1). Teach your dog as many exercises as possible, using our non-forceful method. This will give your dog some 'work' to do and will make it more content.
3. Allow your dog to move towards another dog but before the lead goes tight, call it back to you and reinforce it with food.
4. Never punish your dog physically by using a correction chain for hedging towards another dog.
5. Read the body language of other dogs and take preventive action (Chapter 6).
6. Never carry a stick to ward off other dogs as this will only increase your dog's aggression.
7. Take your dog for long walks.

CHAINED AGGRESSION

8. Do not confine your dog to the garden. Give it free access to you in the house. If necessary, put in a doggy door (Problem 18). This will diminish its interest in other dogs in the neighbourhood. What it can't hear, it won't respond to.

NOTE: Desexing male dogs may have an effect, especially if the surgery is performed early in the dog's life, that is prior to sexual maturity at approximately eight months of age.

From our observations, dogs show variable responses to castration. Some show little, if any, change whilst others alter their behaviour quite considerably. Primarily, it seems to affect their desire to investigate other animals. It also alters their odour so that other male animals react to them in a different way with various results.

AGGRESSION TOWARDS PEOPLE

A dog which is aggressive towards people should only be treated by an experienced professional dog trainer who is familiar with modern behavioural modification techniques and who **only** uses positive reinforcement. Using force or punishing an aggressive dog will only escalate the problem and is **downright dangerous.**

Sometimes drugs prescribed by a veterinarian are used while the dog's behaviour is being re-conditioned. Medication is not effective on its own but makes it easier, and safer, to treat the dog effectively.

Not all aggressive dogs can be treated by a dog trainer. Aggression can be caused by physical conditions such as a brain tumour which must be dealt with medically.

We do not advise anyone to attempt to treat a dog which is aggressive towards people. Professional advice **must** be sought.

B. Mistaken intentions!

CAUSE

+ The body language of some dogs is disguised by excessive facial and body hair, docked tails, altered ear carriage and changes in overall body size.

There are some dogs that other dogs seem to pick on without any provocation. Often the physical appearance of these dogs can actually stimulate aggression. If you were a dog and saw another dog trotting towards you with its neck and rump hair standing up, ears pricked and tail erect, you would be entitled to think it meant business – maybe rough business! You could be very wrong. There are dogs who permanently look like that, for example Finnish Spitz, Samoyeds and Skipperkes. They are not breeds recognised for their aggression, but the dog looking at them may not realise this!

PREVENTION AND CURE

1. Recognise that you might have a breed that could stir up the pugnacious side of another dog!
2. Clipping dogs changes their appearance, which could modify the reaction of a would-be aggressor.

MISTAKEN INTENTIONS

C. Survival of the fittest

CAUSE

● Aggression may result if a group of dogs congregate in a small area or two dogs have to pass each other in a narrow passageway where they feel unable to escape.

● Dogs may compete for something desirable such as a bone.

● When two dogs in a group fight, others in the group generally get involved by rushing in and snapping, or standing on the sidelines barking. Much of the group's aggression is directed towards the dog that appears to be losing the fight. This would be a natural way of supporting the fittest and strongest, thereby sustaining a better gene pool. Humans behave in a similar way when supporting successful athletes. They applaud and parade the winners and just let the losers disappear.

PREVENTION AND CURE

It is good for your dog to mix and socialise with other dogs. However, when dogs congregate in a large group the result can be a melee. At a club which David founded called The Kintala Club, the members are

Investigatory   Ingestive   Eliminative   Care Seeking   Shelter Seeking   Agonistic

encouraged to let their dogs mix without restraint and run together. It is not unusual to see forty to fifty dogs interacting in a multitude of ways. It is a fabulous sight. When members congregate around the coffee table their dogs seem to like to do the same thing! This bunching together stresses some of the dogs and brief scuffles sometimes eventuate. The members are constantly reminded not to stay in large groups for this reason. When they spread out, confrontations are rare.

Often a large party of members and their dogs go for a walk through the parklands beside a winding river, with all the dogs off lead. The natural result is a myriad of happy canine interactions.

These are the rules we have learned at the club:

1. Don't let your dogs mill around in a restricted spot for any length of time.
2. Avoid passing another dog in a doorway or any narrow space.
3. Don't stand too close to other dog owners. Give the dogs room to run freely amongst you.
4. Be prepared to call your dog away from the other dogs from time to time and reinforce it with a piece of food intermittently.

HAPPY DAYS

D. *A change of status*

CAUSE

+ + Some dogs spend a great deal of their lives in the back garden. It is little wonder that two or more dogs living in this isolated type of environment eventually clash. Invariably, the one that loses the fight will be on the lowest rung of the pecking order.

● Sometimes there is just the odd skirmish usually over a bone or another valued object.

● Dogs naturally establish hierarchies if they live in the same group. Older dogs are usually superior to younger ones until they become physically unable to maintain their status.

Status conflicts between two or more dogs who are owned by the same person are not inevitable. David had three entire male miniature Schnauzers who all lived to a ripe old age. They never had a contest for supremacy between them. Their lifestyle was one of sharing. They ate together, slept in the same big bed, had free access to their human family via a doggy door, and were taken for regular walks. There was no reason for confrontation between them.

There are occasions when dogs that have lived peacefully together for many years suddenly become aggressive. Relations of ours had three Border Collies, one male and two female, and one female Golden Retriever. They spent many idyllic years on a thirty acre property with a large dam where they could swim regularly. All was bliss until one of the female Border Collies started to harass the Retriever, who up to that point had been a passive boss lady. Within a few days a major confrontation took place. The Retriever was first to break off the encounter and never asserted herself over the others again. A short time later the Retriever was diagnosed as having inoperable cancer. A likely explanation of these events would be that the Border Collie was able to detect a diminishing physical ability in the Retriever long before her owners became aware of her condition. The natural selection process for group survival had taken place. The fittest must lead.

Many people think that owners should not interfere when a dog is trying to establish superiority over another. 'Let them sort it out' is the usual comment.

The situation that occurred between the three Border Collies and the Retriever on the thirty acre property was very close to the natural behaviour one would observe in the wild. However, the average suburban garden and home does not produce a natural environment. The multitude of hidden stresses that are imposed on dogs magnifies the possibility of aggression within a group. Remove the stresses and you remove most of the hostilities.

PREVENTION

1. Do not create a competitive situation by giving the dogs bones, sticks or balls when they are in close proximity to one another. Space them out well and remove them when the dogs are finished with them.

2. Take the dogs for long walks off lead in a park to enable them to interact peaceably in a large area.

3. When a change in status occurs between two or more dogs it is better to acknowledge the new pecking order by greeting and feeding the dogs in their order of superiority with the highest ranking being fed first.

CURE

1. Teach each dog the 'recall' (Exercise 1) and the 'sit in front' as shown on the opposite page.

2. Having thoroughly conditioned each dog to respond as an individual, you can then signal several dogs to 'come' together and sit facing you. Give a piece of food to each one.

3. Move away from them and repeat the procedure. Repetition of this exercise will not only establish a good recall response, but each dog will find the close proximity of other dogs highly beneficial. In other words, the dogs will think 'I need the presence of other dogs to get a piece of food' rather than 'I'll fight any dog that gets close to my owner!'

   If you teach the dogs to stay while they sit in front of you, you will enhance your control (Exercise 3).

THE RESULT — HARMONY

E. Finders keepers

CAUSE

● The saying 'Possession is nine-tenths of the law' applies to dogs as well as humans. Dogs, however, have little need to own many things. A bone seems to stir the possessive instinct more than anything else.

● Water in a bowl is not something they can call their own and they readily share it with another dog. In any case, they are not motivated to fight over water as it is normally freely available. A piece of meat in the same bowl will invariably arouse the instinct to possess, to eat, to survive.

+ Brook, our gentle, passive Golden Retriever, shows little animosity towards other dogs except when they approach a certain bag which we use when track-

ing. She has learnt that its contents (the harness, tracking lead, articles to find and marking sticks) are collectively associated with a highly beneficial activity which she has learnt to enjoy. In her mind, another dog approaching the bag could jeopardise her pleasure. Her quiet growl seems to do the trick.

+ It may surprise some readers to learn that the breed of dog that comes to us most frequently for behavioural modification due to problems associated with possessive aggression is none other than that lovely cuddly dog, the Cocker Spaniel. For some obscure reason, this basically good-natured dog often hates to give up its ball, stick, bone or other toys; nor

THE *Sit in Front* EXERCISE
INITIAL CONDITIONING

1. Call your dog. As it comes close to you, place your right hand, containing food, in front of the dog's nose.

2. Draw this hand in a flowing motion towards your legs and then up to approximately waist height, bringing your body upright at the same time. This will cause the dog to look up and fall into the sit position.

3. Say 'sit' once only, as soon as the dog starts to adopt the sit position.

4. Reinforce the dog with food from your hand the moment its bottom reaches the ground.

5. Remove your hand quickly back to its original position at waist height.

6. Repeat points 1–5 until the dog's behaviour becomes predictable.

Maintain conditioning by eliminating food in your hand as a stimulus and reinforcing your dog intermittently with food from your pocket.

RESENTMENT

WILLINGNESS

does it like to give up its favourite resting spot. Simply pushing it gently off a chair can lead to a great deal of resentment on the dog's part. Snarls, curled lips, nips and even bites can result.

The simple solution is to find a way which makes the dog *want* to give up the articles or its comfortable chair. Using punishment will only compound the problem. The dog will growl more, snatch and run off with articles and become more menacing when approached. The same can be said of verbal chastisement such as 'No' or 'Bad dog'. **Aggression only promotes aggression.**

PREVENTION

From the time a puppy or dog is first brought into the home it should be taught to retrieve articles and give them up as shown in Exercise 5.

If the dog is occupying a chair, encourage it to jump down by placing your hand, containing a piece of food, on the floor just in front of the chair. Make sure the food is obvious to the dog. As it jumps down say 'Down'. The moment it reaches your hand give it the piece of food. Repeat this whenever the opportunity arises. Once the dog has learnt the response, reinforce it intermittently.

HOLD AND GIVE

GIVE AND TAKE

CURE

Curing the problem of a dog which will not give things up involves a similar technique to teaching retrieving. However, your actions and timing must inhibit any *thought* of aggression in the dog.

1. Hold an article in one hand and a piece of food in the other.

2. Encourage the dog to take the article in its mouth but do not release it from your hand.

3. Present the food to the dog saying the word 'Give'.

4. As the dog releases the article, give it the food.

Repeat this procedure until the dog eagerly releases the article. Then do the same thing with the article at ground level, but still held in your hand. Repeat this several times. Continue to reinforce this passive response when you place the article on the ground.

With regard to possessiveness over the dog's food bowl, it is best to start with a bowl of food which is held at the dog's nose level. Offer several pieces of food by hand. Then remove the bowl for several seconds before returning it to a position 5 to 10 centimetres below the dog's nose. Feed again by hand. Repeat this procedure, gradually lowering the bowl until it reaches ground level. The dog will become quite prepared to accept your participation in its eating routine.

The problem of a dog which actually bites people who come near its food is dealt with in food-related problems (Problem 6D).

PROBLEM *13* ON THE CHASE

When an animal is triggered into either chasing or fleeing, it is oblivious to all that is going on around it. This makes chasing an extremely dangerous behaviour in suburbia, because the dog may run out in front of a car and get killed or injured. It may cause vehicles to collide, killing or injuring the driver or passengers. If an animal is being chased, it is likely to suffer the same fate (Problem 10B).

In outer urban areas packs of dogs sometimes chase livestock who may be slaughtered, die of fright or abort their young.

CAUSE

● Some breeds such as sight hounds and herding dogs are more readily triggered by movement.

● It is a strong innate behaviour for dogs to chase, catch and kill in order to survive.

● ● Groups of dogs can become so excited by the chase that they may kill more animals than they could eat. This would rarely happen in the wild as the majority of their prey could flee and escape. Domestic livestock are restrained by walls or fences, which makes them particularly vulnerable to attack. Their lack of experience and physical fitness also reduces their chances of escape compared to their wild counterparts.

PREVENTION

1. The most obvious preventive strategy is **never** to allow your dog to chase animals or any type of moving machinery.
2. Choose a breed of dog carefully according to your circumstances, rather than because you like the look of it. Many gun dogs and loose-lipped breeds such as Great Danes, Mastiffs and St Bernards are generally placid and less likely to exhibit hunting behaviour. Small dogs such as Bishon Frise, Cavalier King Charles Spaniels, Dachshunds, Maltese Terriers and Pomeranians are unlikely to be able to inflict much damage on livestock and their size inhibits them from moving too fast and going far.

SOCIALISATION WITH SHEEP

SOCIALISATION WITH CATTLE

Investigatory   Ingestive   Eliminative   Care Seeking   Shelter Seeking   Agonistic

Greyhounds, Whippets and Terriers show an inclination to attack small animals such as cats, chickens and rabbits. Basenjis and Siberian Huskies are closer in behaviour to the wolf and given the opportunity will quickly revert back to normal hunting behaviour. Huskies are also capable of covering long distances in a short time. Herding breeds such as Border Collies, Kelpies and Heelers are more likely to dash after and 'herd' cars and motorcycles. The fact that these breeds often work on farming properties also gives them greater opportunities to chase and hunt animals. Professional farmers are well aware of this, but pet owners who live in the country do not always realise their dogs' potential.

3. Dogs should be introduced under supervision to any species of animal with which they are likely to come in contact during their lifetime, e.g. cats, chickens, cows, horses and sheep. It is important that this occurs when they are pups during their critical socialisation period, particularly if they are going to live in a rural area. However, if you have just moved to the country with an older dog, you should go through a similar socialisation procedure, taking particular care that your dog cannot chase the animals. Put it on a long lead such as a horse's lunging rein to make sure this does not happen.

In some places dogs, e.g. the Pyrenean Mountain Dog, Komondor and Maremma are actually raised with sheep so that they regard the flock as their 'pack'.

4. Make sure that your dog is left in a secure garden or run when you have to go out. This will prevent it joining packs of other dogs and hunting your neighbour's livestock or roaming the streets and getting run over. If your dog cannot get into the house through a doggy door (Problem 18) it will need shade in summer, shelter in winter and water all the year round.

CURE

Once your dog has been reinforced by the thrill of the chase, the behaviour is almost impossible to eradicate completely. However, there are a number of things which you can do to **control** the situation **when you are present.**

1. Teach your dog to come when called, first in a restricted environment and then in open spaces (Exercise 1).

2. Teach it to 'sit' and 'sit stay' (Exercises 2 and 3).

3. Next, take your dog into the situation which stimulated the chasing behaviour.

Now go on to A, below, or B on page 102.

A. Horses, sheep and other farm animals

4. Choose one or two bold cows, horses, sheep or other animals which will not run when faced with a dog.

5. Place a long lead of 3 to 5 metres on your dog and take it close to the animals. Put your dog in a sit position and reinforce it a few times for remaining still.

6. Repeat 5 with the animals moving slowly.

7. Gradually increase the number and speed of the animals and reinforce your dog *intermittently* for staying in the sit position. Practise this until you feel confident enough to remove the lead.

    Always monitor the dog's behaviour with animals or it may quickly revert back to chasing them.

B. Bicycles, cars and motorbikes

4. Take your dog outside on a long light lead and place it in a sit stay position on the pavement.
   NOTE: The lead is used as a safety precaution for your dog, not as a training aid.

5. Condition your dog not to chase vehicles in just the same way as we conditioned them not to chase animals. First get a friend to ride a bicycle **slowly** past the dog while you reinforce it in the sit position.

6. Gradually increase the speed of the bicycle, reinforcing your dog for staying still.

7. Repeat the same procedure with a car and motorcycle, making your reinforcements intermittent so that your dog cannot predict when it is going to be fed. Repeat this procedure until you are confident that your dog is conditioned not to chase vehicles when you are present.
   Never give your dog the opportunity to chase vehicles again! It is impossible to eliminate such natural inborn traits. Prevention is the key!

C. Cats

Chasing cats can be dealt with in the same way as other animals such as horses or sheep, but if your dog chases your own cat, the following procedure will nearly always produce a sustained cure. You can also use this method when introducing your cat and dog to each other.

1. Make sure both animals are hungry by delaying their meal time for a few hours.

2. Choose a place where you can feed them with the cat placed in a high position above the dog, e.g. cat on a bench, dog on the floor. Place their bowls of food down at the same time and monitor the situation as they eat.

3. Repeat this *every* time the cat and dog eat, gradually bringing them closer together as they feed. This will ensure that the animals see each other as beneficial. Eating together will also make your dog perceive the cat as a member of its social group.

THE THINGS WE DO IN LIFE!

PROBLEM *14* **A** FOUR-LEGGED DEMOLITION SQUAD

Destructive behaviour takes many forms, from chewing up a few pot plants to total destruction of an entire room. It is probably one of the major causes of premature death in the canine population, because many dog owners think that having the dog destroyed is the only solution. However, there are literally dozens of things which can be done to prevent, or at least minimise the problem. As always, the solution entails commitment to, and involvement with, the dog.

CAUSE

+ Boredom is the number one cause of destructive behaviour. The lives of many suburban backyard dogs are severely deficient of opportunities to explore and socialise.

Young dogs who are teething will frequently chew on any hard material which is available to relieve the pain in their gums. They don't know the difference between an expensive table leg or any other piece of wood!

● Playing tug of war excessively with an excitable dog or with a breed which has a genetically inherited tendency to hang on to things (e.g. terriers) will make a dog much more likely to play tug of war with household curtains, mats, etc!

PREVENTION AND CURE

1. Read Problem 1 and put into practice any of the recommendations which you feel would be useful in your situation. Put the obvious articles which dogs like chewing such as pot plants out of reach.
2. Do not play tug of war with excitable dogs.
3. Provide chew toys, changing them regularly to maintain your dog's interest.
4. Fence off newly planted areas in the garden temporarily.
5. Teach your dog to retrieve as shown in Exercise 5 to amuse and exercise it. Dog-owners who cannot walk far can give their dogs a good run in this way. If your dog is not interested in picking things up in its mouth, you can create an eagerness to retrieve by following the suggestions in *Dog Training — The Gentle Modern Method*.

   Retrieving is a particularly useful exercise for disabled owners who cannot bend to pick things up, and a number of dogs are currently being trained specifically for this purpose.

THE WRECKE

CAUSE

Dogs dig holes for a variety of reasons:

 (a) To bury bones or surplus food.

 (b) To keep cool during hot weather. The holes may be in the open or under the house or a tree, but they are usually dug in sandy or soft soil.

 (c) A bitch may create a hollowed area to prepare for the birth of her pups. She may even attempt to dig a 'hole' in the carpet.

 (d) To escape from boredom or confinement, e.g. digging out under a fence to give the dog the opportunity to investigate further afield, or simply digging holes to amuse itself because there is nothing else to do!

 (e) Both male and female dogs may dig out of an enclosed area to reach a member of the opposite sex when the bitch is in season.

ESCAPE FROM BOREDOM

PREVENTION AND CURE

Preventing the problems associated with normal canine behaviour is fairly easy, see a, b and c.

a

If we allow a dog to chew on a bone for fifteen minutes or so and then take away what is left, the dog will have little opportunity, or need, to dig a hole to store the surplus.

Of course there are some dogs who don't try to eat a bone but immediately take it away and attempt to bury it. This may be because the dog is satiated and does not require any more food, or it may be the result of stress. Stress is usually due to the presence of other dogs or people which the dog finds threatening because they might attempt to take the bone away. This can be prevented by providing the dog with a quiet area where there is no competition.

Obviously if the dog is not hungry enough to want a bone or is burying excess food, the solution is to feed it less often or offer smaller amounts. Appropriate feeding regimes for healthy puppies and dogs are discussed in Problem 6.

b

Curing the problem of a dog which digs holes to keep cool is also fairly simple. You should make sure that the dog has free access to a cool shady area at all times of the day, be it under the house, on a sheltered verandah or by letting it go in and out of the house when it wants to via a doggy door (Problem 18). Like people, some elderly dogs become particularly stressed by heat, especially if they have breathing problems.

c

A bitch which is due to have puppies in a matter of days should be introduced to her 'birthing area' well before the event so that she becomes accustomed to it. She should be supervised when she is outside so that she does not begin to prepare, what we might consider, an unsuitable den. To fulfil her inborn drive to prepare a den, she can be provided with paper which she can tear up in the whelping area. A bitch will often use this to create a hollow place and this should help to stop her drive to dig holes in the carpet!

d

Dealing with a dog that digs because it is bored or confined requires a much greater commitment on the part of the dog owner, because the solution involves a considerable amount of effort (Problem 1). It involves activities which every dog needs such as taking it for a daily walk with at least some time off lead, and making sure it has regular contact with the family. However, all dog owners should be doing these things whether the dogs have a problem or not. People who are not prepared to cater for a dog's basic needs should not own a dog. We owe them much more than food, water and the occasional pat on the head as we go about our busy lives.

e

Entire male dogs have a natural drive to go looking for a mate, a tendency shared by bitches during estrus. Male dogs have a much bigger problem than wolves because female dogs come into season at different times of the year and have seasons more frequently, so there may be receptive bitches to attract him during most of the year! Both sexes may be so determined that little will deter them from getting out, one way or another. Once a dog has dug out in one area it will tend to return to that spot again.

Castration or speying may appear to be the answer to this problem but this raises an ethical question: are we desexing dogs to suit ourselves or because it is of benefit to the dog? I think you would agree that in most cases we do it because it makes life easier for us! There are other effective strategies to use which will help to lessen a dog's desire to escape and look for a mate, and it is *absolutely imperative* that you use them if you choose to have an entire male or female dog (see Problem 1). With many thousands of dogs being destroyed each year in most countries around the world, we cannot afford to be responsible for yet another unplanned litter. We will discuss how to avoid an unwanted pregnancy in Problem 26.

Remember that both sexes will be much less likely to dig out if they are not bored.

PROBLEM *16* **H**ANGING ON THE WASHING

FLAPPING FUN

CAUSE

● Some dogs are highly stimulated by movement and find washing flapping in the breeze much more exciting than the static toys which may be provided for them.

✚ Dogs who are not given enough opportunity to exercise and explore regularly will be much more likely to seek out other sources of amusement. Hanging on the washing is a classic boredom-related problem.

● Once a dog has latched onto a piece of material hanging from the line, the resistance will tend to make it pull even harder! The behaviour can be likened to killing prey.

PREVENTION

1. Prevent your dog from becoming bored by putting the recommendations in Problem 1 into practice.
2. Monitor your dog on the first few occasions when you put the washing out. Puppies may not be able to reach any of the clothes that are hanging down, so you will have to watch out for the moment when your dog is likely to be large enough to do any damage. Always try to prevent the behaviour from starting, otherwise your dog will be highly reinforced by this great game of tug of war.
3. Never leave washing flapping near the dog's eye level.
4. Avoid playing tug of war, especially if you have a breed which is recognised for its tendency to hang on, e.g. terriers.

CURE

1. The obvious solution to the problem is not to leave washing out when your dog cannot be supervised at least to begin with, or alternatively to hang it out in an area to which the dog does not have access.
2. If this is impractical you can foil the dog by placing a few bricks on the ground below the clothes

Investigatory | Ingestive | Eliminative | Care Seeking | Shelter Seeking | Agonistic

TENTATIVE TOES

line and laying wire mesh on top of them. Your dog is most unlikely to walk on this type of surface.

When the pattern of behaviour has been stopped for a few weeks, you can probably take the wire and bricks away. Try this first of all when you are at home and can surreptitiously watch what happens!

3. You can use something with a pungent smell such as oil of citronella to make the washing on the line less attractive. Sprinkle this oil on an old rag and let your dog sniff it. If it immediately steps away, this will suggest that it dislikes the odour. Impregnate a few pieces of rag with the oil and hang them on the line much lower than any of the 'good' washing. A dog is more likely to investigate things which are closer to the ground so the pungent smell may deter further investigation.

However, there are many dogs that find any smell appealing! If you own one of these odour eaters, then this method will have little effect.

NOTE: Many people mistakenly think that their dog looks 'guilty' when they return home to find washing torn off the line. In fact, the dog is either reacting to their body language which it reads as angry, or it is drawing an association between the owner's homecoming and being punished in the past. It therefore takes up a submissive posture in an unconscious effort to appease.

Dogs are not capable of relating punishment to a 'crime' unless the two occur almost simultaneously. Therefore it is absolutely useless to punish a dog hours, or even minutes after it has done something 'wrong'. Dogs have no concept of right and wrong and never do things 'to annoy' or 'get even'. Simply take responsibility for the problem yourself and go about resolving it in a logical way which takes into consideration your dog's limited cognitive abilities and your substantial fund of knowledge.

PROBLEM *17* **R**OUND THE BEND?

– COMPULSIVE BEHAVIOUR IN DOGS

Some examples of compulsive behaviour are:

1. Excessive drinking or playing with water, e.g. upsetting bowls of water or paddling the front feet in a water bucket.
2. Stone chewing and swallowing.
3. Snapping at, or pouncing on, imaginary objects.
4. Compulsive licking and/or chewing, sometimes to the point of exposing the dog's own bone.
5. Tail chasing.
6. Dogs that constantly pad up and down the fence line in a bizarre manner.
7. Constant barking for no apparent reason.

FRENZY!

Investigatory   Ingestive   Eliminative   Care Seeking   Shelter Seeking   Agonistic

CAUSE

Most of the behaviours mentioned in the examples above originally started because there was a genuine stimulus which promoted them, e.g. a dog may lick or chew itself because it is itchy or it may bark because it sees something. Later, such behaviour can become habit formed and occur whether a stimulus is present or not.

✛ A lack of opportunity to explore and exercise naturally due to confinement often leads to boredom and the dog then seeks ways in which to entertain itself, e.g. playing with water.

✛ The anatomy of some dogs (e.g. Bull Terriers) is such that they find it difficult to raise their heads high to look out over a wide vista. These types of breeds are more likely to concentrate on what goes on below their eye level and therefore they are more stimulated to chase their own tails.

PREVENTION

Read Problem 1 on how to prevent boredom in your dog and put the recommended strategies into practice. In particular, provide your dog with regular exercise and involve it in family life.

CURE

1. First of all check that there is no physical reason for the compulsive behaviour. For example, excessive drinking may be due to diabetes, kidney failure or an infection, and excessive licking may be due to an allergic reaction.
2. Remove stones from your garden if you have a stone chewing dog, or place the dog in a different area where there are no stones. An obvious solution but one which is not always put into practice!
3. If your dog tips over its water bowl, dig a hole and set a bucket of water into it so that it can be easily removed for cleaning.
4. The use of an automatic tap connected with the drinking bowl will foil the antics of the dog who likes to paddle in buckets of water.
5. Needless to say, none of these cures will work if you do not deal with the underlying cause! Anything which improves your dog's quality of life and is reasonably practical must be considered.

    (a) Do not confine your dog to a small enclosure. Animals in cages quickly develop stereotyped patterns of behaviour.

    (b) Leave different toys out each day.

    (c) Consider providing a companion.

    (d) Teach your dog a number of obedience exercises, in particular retrieving (Exercise 5) which provides exercise as well as mental stimulation.

Recent research in the USA has likened behaviours such as self-mutilating licking with obsessive compulsive disorder in humans. Scientists suggest that there may be an underlying biological cause such as the excessive production of dopamine. (Dopamine is a neurotransmitter in the brain.) They have been experimenting by giving such dogs drugs which reduce dopamine production. It appears that the behaviour improves while the drugs are taken, but regresses when treatment ceases. We mention this because it may be advisable to consult your veterinarian about drug treatment if all else fails. However, we strongly recommend that you put a great deal of effort into behavioural therapy before resorting to medication.

CAUSE

＋ Confinement and lack of social contact may result in dogs becoming excessively excited by any external stimulus such as the dog next-door running up and down the fence line. Excitement often leads to barking.

● Wolves do not bark at prey as they do not want to make their presence known. Dogs such as the Siberian Husky have inherited this trait and rarely if ever develop a barking problem. Basenjis don't bark although they sometimes let out one woof; they howl instead!

＋ Humans have genetically selected dogs for an increased tendency to bark, sometimes unconsciously, and sometimes for specific purposes such as guarding. Herding dogs have a propensity to excessive barking as this helps to move sheep or cattle along the trail.

＋ Puppies learn to bark when they are young because they are stimulated to do so by hearing other dogs bark.

● The sounds of a dog barking will often activate barking in other dogs in the same neighbourhood in a chain reaction.

PREVENTION

It is important to realise that most cases of excessive barking occur as a result of boredom and that if you follow all the advice suggested in Problem 1 the problem should not develop. For instance, you will notice that when you take your dog for a walk in the park, it rarely barks.

The socialisation of a young puppy is particularly important to ensure that it is less excited and stimulated by new events. Well socialised pups have an attitude of 'been there, done that' and the result is that they are less likely to be excited by life in general, see Chapter 2 on How to bring up the perfect dog.

CURE

There are a number of things which you can do if you already have the problem of a barking dog. The first and most important solution is to keep the dog inside whenever possible so that it is less stimulated by what is going on outside. You may be able to organise a neighbour to take your dog out to urinate and defecate at least once during the day if you go out. Many neighbours would actually prefer to do this rather than listen to a constant bark, bark, bark! This type of interaction may also improve relations between you and your neighbour and your neighbour and your dog! If it is impossible to arrange for someone to take your dog out, then you should seriously consider putting in a doggy door as shown in the photograph.

Other strategies include feeding the dog in the morning and providing a sheltered area so that the dog is more likely to sleep or rest for part of the day.

COME AND GO AT WIL

| Investigatory | Ingestive | Eliminative | Care Seeking | Shelter Seeking | Agonistic |

THE CANINE ESCAPOLOGISTS!

CAUSE

✛ This problem is also related to boredom (Problem 1). Dogs are constantly stimulated by sounds, smells and sights outside their own garden, but they are usually prevented from investigating them.

Imagine being a prisoner of war, or being in jail. The high fences, the guards and the confinement would make you feel desperate. Relief from tedium would often be expressed in ways which would make the jailers stressed and angry. The bizarre actions of prisoners, such as wrecking their cells and pacing up and down, are the result of a natural, but frustrated, desire to be free.

The behavioural patterns that usually develop in a dog that suffers confinement are similar to those of human prisoners. First the wrecking of garden items such as the hose, broom or pot plants (Problem 14), then pacing up and down beside the fence (Problem 17) and finally the attempt to escape.

How do dogs escape?

A. *Digging under the fence*

A dog will often dig near the fence at a point where the neighbour's dog goes frequently. The two dogs may be stimulated by the sight of one another through a slight gap in the palings or between the bottom of the fence and the ground. Perhaps your neighbour has dug some beautiful smelling compost into the ground or the dog has buried a bone nearby. All these things make digging even more enjoyable!

THE GREAT ESCAPE 1

Investigatory | Ingestive | Eliminative | Care Seeking | Shelter Seeking | Agonistic

PREVENTION

Boredom is a major cause of escape behaviour. The dog simply does not have enough to do to keep itself amused. We advise you to act on some of the suggestions in Problem 1 so that you can prevent any escape behaviour from developing in the first place.

CURE

There are a number of non aversive ways to deter your dog from digging, some more costly and time consuming than others:

1. Redesign the area into a rockery.
2. Place a temporary wire fence around the area so that the dog cannot reach the fence. Changing the environment can change the behaviour.
3. Place chicken wire on the ground adjacent to the fence and weigh it down with bricks or timber.

B. Jumping out

When one dog sees or hears another on the other side of a fence, the two dogs do not sit back and evaluate the situation to discover the easiest way of reaching one another. They usually run up and down the fence line for a short distance and then try to scale the fence close to where the other dog is situated. It does not occur to them to look for a gap or a low spot in the fence. The need to get to one another makes them take the most direct route. Once a dog has successfully escaped at one point, it will tend to jump out at that point again because it has been rewarded for doing so in the past.

CURE

All animals must approach a jump at the right speed and angle in order to thrust their body up and over. Our solution to the jumping problem therefore relies on spoiling the dog's ability to 'take off'. This can be done in three ways.

1. Scatter a few rocks or bricks on the ground where the dog jumps and cover these with chicken wire. Many dogs will be deterred by this uneven surface.
2. Slope the garden or lawn down towards the fence. This will prevent the dog from running and springing up. However, it is labour intensive and not very aesthetically pleasing.

3. The most efficient deterrent of all is one we have recommended many times with great success, and the one which cured an established canine 'Houdini'. It involves running a strong taut horizontal wire parallel to the fence and about 30 centimetres out from it, as shown in the photograph. The wire can be attached to strong stakes driven into the ground or to battens attached to the fence. The wire must be situated at a height which interferes with the dog's line of flight. This will obviously depend on the size and agility of the particular animal and should be assessed carefully before construction begins! If you use this preventive system you will avoid the necessity of building higher and higher fences.

THE PERMANENT GUARD

THE GREAT ESCAPE 2

C. Squeezing out

Some dogs develop a 'now you see me, now you don't' reaction when a door or gate is opened slightly. They squeeze out of the narrow opening and take off like mercury escaping from a thermometer. It is a funny quirk of human and animal nature that the moment something is not allowed, it becomes more desirable! The partly opened door or gate acts as a trigger for the dog to want to go and investigate.

CURE

1. The first solution is easy, but may not be practical! Simply open the door or gate wide and let the dog out to explore for a while — provided it is safe of course! After a short time call your dog back to you (Exercise 1). Your dog will soon become blasé about the whole situation.

2. The second solution is to teach your dog to sit and stay as you open the door or gate and then allow it to move away on signal (Exercises 2 and 3).

REFLECTIONS ON LIFE

20 PET ME TO DEATH, PLEASE DO!

CAUSE

+ Attention-seeking behaviour, such as excessive whining, barking, pawing, begging and smooching, are simply an extension of the normal care-seeking behaviour exhibited by young wolf cubs and puppies.

+ We actually discourage our dogs from becoming adult in their behaviour and instead create and reinforce their dependence on us by such actions as:

1. Frequently lifting pups on our laps when they are small.
2. Carrying pups or small dogs in our arms because we are frightened they might get hurt.

OVER PROTECTIVENESS

3. Letting a pup in the house whenever it barks or whines outside or giving it a biscuit in an attempt to make it quiet.
4. Stroking it when it licks our face or paws at us. (This is a direct throw back to licking or pawing adult wolves to stimulate regurgitation.)
5. Encouraging pups to jump up on our legs and stroking them for doing so.

Often we regard these types of behaviours as cute in puppyhood but not so desirable in an adult dog. A large dog trying to sit on our lap may not be very welcome. A dog that constantly begs at the table or helps itself to the barbeque will not be invited out again!

Personally, we like our dogs to come up to us for a stroke and cuddle as we regard this as one of the many pleasures of sharing our lives with them. But it is up to you to decide what you will allow and what is taboo in your household. Provided your dog lives a happy fulfilled life, a few rules are of benefit rather than being detrimental. But . . . what should you do if your dog is unacceptably demanding?

PREVENTION AND CURE

1. The golden rule is consistency from everyone who comes in contact with the dog. Make the rules about the dog's code of conduct and stick to them, otherwise the dog will become totally confused.
2. If you have a young dog we suggest that you read Chapter 2 on how to bring up the perfect dog and put our recommendations into practice.
3. Never feed your dog at the table unless you want it to beg or wait expectantly at every meal. Intermittent reinforcement in the form of the occasional titbit will only strengthen this behaviour.
4. When you leave the dog outside, only invite it in when it is quiet and never when it is whining, barking or scratching at the door. A doggy door is the best option for the dog so that it can come and go at will, see Problem 18.
5. Ignore your dog if it paws, whimpers or smooches up to you — if you don't want that to happen — or go into another room for a *very short* time.
6. Provide alternative activities, particularly playing with other dogs or people, so that it becomes less reliant on you.
7. Exercise and train your dog regularly so that it is happy to rest at the end of the day.
8. Avoid being overly protective, particularly of puppies and small dogs. Let them explore and find out about the world so that they are well socialised.

CAUSE

● It is natural for pups to mount other puppies from an early age. The sexual act is incomplete, but in all probability it feels pleasant. In a wolf pack only bold superior wolves will breed and this is probably why the behaviour is more common in young dominant male dogs.

● Females in estrus will often mount other females.

● Males find the pheromones of a bitch in season very attractive and are strongly stimulated to mount her.

+ Dogs will also mount humans, particularly members of their own family group. They may be more likely to do this if they have been primarily socialised with humans rather than with other dogs.

+ Castrated males may also exhibit mounting behaviour, particularly if the habit was well established before desexing took place.

PREVENTION AND CURE

1. Try to anticipate and prevent mounting behaviour by taking note of the situations which prompted it in the past.
2. Keep entire male dogs completely away from bitches in season and their secretions.
3. Avoid generating any behaviour which encourages jumping up (Problem 3).
4. Take part in training or activities which increase the handlers 'superiority' over the dog, e.g. teaching the dog to 'sit stay' (Exercise 3) or drop, see *Dog Training: The Gentle Modern Method*.

   NOTE: The use of the word 'superior' does **not** imply that force should be used. People are vastly superior to dogs intellectually and should **never** have to employ physical dominance.
5. Avoid scratching the base of the dog's tail or other erogenous zones!
6. If a dog mounts someone, the person should not get angry, but quietly stop the dog and then create a diversion by taking part in an activity which the dog enjoys, preferably something active like retrieving, or going for a walk. People must make sure their clothes do not carry odours which are likely to stimulate a sexual response in the dog.

22 THE ONE WOMAN (OR ONE MAN) DOG!

CAUSE

In spite of the fact that 'one man dog' is a fairly common expression, the 'one woman dog' seems to be more common in our society! Perhaps this is because women traditionally spend more time working at home and consequently spend more time with the family dog. Perhaps many women are inherently more gentle with animals than men and this results in the woman of the house being more beneficial in the dog's eyes.

David was consulted about a dog that wouldn't allow a man to get into bed with his wife. This type of situation can lead to a great deal of marital disharmony and ultimately to the divorce courts!

Similar problems can arise when one or more family members become concerned because their dog seems to prefer others in the family and does not respond to them. The situation can escalate to a point where some family members may no longer want the dog.

CURE

Like many problems in life, the solution involves a bit of time and effort in conjunction with some changes in attitude from all members of the family concerned. In turn, this will lead to a change in attitude in the dog. Take, for example, the case of the dog who growls and bites the husband when he attempts to get into bed with his wife. Looking at it from the dog's point of view, the husband is synonymous with having to relinquish its warm comfortable position on the bed.

A 'superior' type of animal will naturally try to maintain its comfortable status by getting rid of its 'competitor'. Many people unfortunately try to solve this problem by the use of punishment, such as hitting the dog or pushing it roughly off the bed. This may work for one night but the punishment will have to be repeated again and again every night and become more and more severe to maintain the dog's response.

The husband may end up by being badly bitten while the dog becomes more and more aggressive.

A lasting solution is to condition the dog to **want** to sleep in a different spot by going through the following process. (Owners of dogs who have not got to the biting stage can start at point 5.)

1. The wife should cease to be of benefit to the dog, i.e. stop feeding, exercising, or showing affection to the dog, for a period of time which will depend upon the severity of the problem. Her husband must take over this role. She should also ignore the dog as much as possible during this period. Given their close relationship, this will be hard for both wife and dog, but if the alternative is divorce or getting rid of the dog altogether, then surely this is a better option.

2. The husband must go out of his way to make a great fuss of the dog and most importantly to feed, exercise and train it.

   Teaching the 'recall' (Exercise 1) will give him the confidence that he can control the dog and call it back to him when he takes it for a walk. The fact that he is reinforcing it with food will make the dog *choose* to respond.

3. Once their relationship has improved, which should only take a matter of days, we suggest that the dog should be given a comfortable bed *beside* the owners' bed. The wife should stay out of the room at this stage. The husband should induce the dog to climb into its own bed by using a piece of food as shown in the photograph. He should then reinforce the dog with its favourite food while it is in its own bed. The process will be even more efficient if the regular meal is withdrawn and the husband feeds the dog a suitable meal by hand while it is in its own bed. Husband and wife can then get into bed.

Investigatory | Ingestive | Eliminative | Care Seeking | Shelter Seeking | Agonistic

4. The next step is for the husband to climb into bed and then call the dog into its own bed close by. Again he should give the dog its meal by hand. When the dog has eaten, the wife can get into bed.

The final procedure should involve the scenario which caused the problem in the first place: wife in bed and dog on the bed. The dog should not have been fed that day.

5. The husband should place his hand, containing food, close to the floor beside the bed making this action obvious to the dog. As the dog jumps off the bed to get the food it is instantly reinforced. The signal 'down' should be given as the dog jumps. The dog should be induced into its own bed and fed there. The husband should then climb into his own bed.

6. Repeat point 5 a few times until the dog is conditioned to go to its own bed. Finally reinforce the dog intermittently while it is in its own bed to maintain this behaviour.

Both husband and wife must be consistent and set the rules for the future and adhere to them. For instance, if the wife allows the dog on the bed when her husband is away, then the whole situation may recur. She can gradually take a more active role in the dog's life again, but it is important that her husband also continues to take part in activities which the dog enjoys.

Poor relationships between a dog and any member of a family can be solved by using a similar procedure.

PROBLEM 23 A CHILD IN THE FAMILY
– NO PROBLEM

A. Introducing your dog to a new baby in the family

Young married couples should think carefully before getting a dog if they intend to start a family in the near future. Not because the dog will be a problem, but because dogs are frequently neglected when a new baby arrives. A new mother is often tired and anxious and the welfare of the dog may be the last thing on her mind. Some parents are also afraid that their dog will attack the child or spread disease.

Personally, we are very much against the idea of relegating the dog to the garden when a baby arrives. However, if you have decided that you are not prepared to have the dog in the house, then you should plan well ahead. Any changes in routine should happen well before the baby comes home so that the dog does not associate the baby with its change of circumstances.

It is infinitely better for your dog to maintain its usual routine as much as possible. Dogs who are allowed to be part of the family will regard a young baby simply as another member of its pack. And, from our knowledge of wolf behaviour, we know that older wolves nurture young members of the pack, they do not attack them!

An excellent relationship will develop between the dog and baby provided the dog does not think that the baby is responsible for having its privileges withdrawn! Nobody responds to that situation favourably! However, interaction between the baby and dog should always be monitored by a responsible person.

We suggest that you deal with the situation in this way:

1. Bring the new baby into the house in some kind of carry cot. Sit your dog beside the cot and reinforce it a few times by offering it a few pieces of food. The smell and sight of the baby will then be associated with great benefit in the dog's mind. The theory that eating meat 'bloods' a dog and makes it aggressive is a fallacy; there is no evidence for it.

2. Next allow the dog to investigate the baby by sniffing it and watching it. Monitor the interaction at all times. Pat the dog and make a fuss of it while the baby is present.

3. When you first pick the baby up in the dog's presence, reinforce the dog again with some pieces of food.

4. Only pat the dog while the baby is present for the first few days until it has had time to get used to the new social structure.

5. Give the dog its meals in the presence of the baby, too, so that all the best things in life happen while the baby is around.

6. When you want to put the dog outside, do so *before* you pick the baby up.

7. Never chastise your dog for picking up the baby's toys. The smell of the baby must never be associated with aversive events! Simply take the toy away and wash it carefully and give the dog one of its *own* toys.

8. When the baby starts to sit up on the floor and crawl make sure that he or she does not pull the dog's hair, ears, etc. to a point where the dog becomes annoyed. It is *natural* for dogs to react to hurt by snapping or biting as a warning. After all, it's the only way they can. It is amazing that the vast majority of dogs are actually so tolerant! But, be warned, dogs do not have morality and injuries, can, and do result when dogs are provoked.

9. As soon as the child is old enough, you should teach him or her how to handle the dog correctly (see page 16). A four to five year old should be quite capable of sitting the dog and then putting

FAMILY LIFE

its meal down for it. Make sure your dog is entirely reliable around its food bowl (Problem 6D). A slightly older child can help with grooming.

NOTE: Make sure that your dog is regularly wormed and groomed and check that it does not have fleas, particularly when you have a small child or children in the house.

Never leave a baby or small child unattended with a strange dog which is not used to children.

B. Introducing a dog into the family

Raising children involves a considerable amount of time and effort as every parent knows. Looking after a dog for its lifetime should involve a similar, if less time-consuming, commitment. There are a few questions the family should consider before taking the first step.

1. Is everyone in the family keen to have a dog? If not, is this likely to cause friction?
2. Should you buy a pure, cross or mixed breed? The type you choose must fit in with the family and your lifestyle. Do your research first by visiting dog shows, talking to breeders and reading books. Our views on the trainability of some breeds of dog are listed in Appendix B.
3. Do you have the time to walk the dog daily and groom it adequately?
4. Are the family finances adequate to meet not only basic requirements such as food, but also unexpected veterinary bills?
5. Who is going to look after the dog if you go away on holiday or can you take it with you?
6. Are you prepared to let the dog be part of the family, i.e. live inside the house with you? Dogs who are left alone outside invariably become very excited when people are around and can become destructive. Children and an excited dog are not a good combination!
7. Do you realise that you are going to have full responsibility for the dog's welfare for ten to fifteen years, or even more?

Once the big decision has been made, the next step is planning for the puppy or older dog's arrival. This is an ideal time to start teaching responsible dog ownership to your childen, primarily by example. Depending on their age, they can help to make fences and gates secure. They can have great fun helping to choose a collar with identification tag, food bowls, worming tablets, the dog's own toys and preparing a snug bed.

We suggest that you set the rules of behaviour for

BEDTIME STORY

ME AND MY PAL

your children and the new dog from the day the latter arrives. Consistency is most important! Encourage the children to help feed, groom, exercise and train the dog, again depending on their age and maturity. All family members should be aware of following points:

1. Puppies need a place of their own to sleep undisturbed frequently during the day.
2. Children, in particular, should avoid wearing shoe laces and loose fitting clothes which are easy for a puppy to grab and pull. This behaviour often becomes a habit (Problem 8).
3. No one should shout or flap their hands around when playing with the new dog. This will encourage excitable behaviour and a tendency for the pup to nip or bite (Problem 11).
4. Small children who lift their hands up to protect their faces will stimulate a young dog to jump up to investigate them. They should be taught to stay fairly passive when the puppy is around and the interaction between them should be monitored at all times. Always remember that moving objects including children will frequently trigger a hunting chase response in dogs (Problem 3).
5. Teenagers, especially boys, can be guilty of boxing dogs around the face while playing. Unwittingly, they may teach the dog to bite. Discourage them at all costs!
6. Playing tug of war can create another problem. A gentle game of tug of war is good for dogs who are not keen to hold onto articles or who need to be encouraged to retrieve and hold things in their mouths. It is *not* advisable for dogs such as Bull Terriers, Staffordshire Bull Terriers and other breeds with extraordinarily powerful jaws which have an in-built propensity to 'hang on'.

C. Your child and other people's dogs

We frequently hear worried parents saying to their children 'don't touch, it might bite you' when they meet a strange dog. Although we can understand their concern, their actions often instil in the child a great fear of dogs which can have unfortunate repercussions. Children should certainly be discouraged from rushing up to dogs which they don't know, and they should never approach and touch any dog from the rear before it has had a chance to see them coming. The best strategy is to teach children to ask owners if their dog is friendly and if they are allowed to pat it. In this way, the child will learn to like dogs but will also realise that some dogs should be avoided.

Children should never be allowed to tease any dog however placid it appears to be. As we mentioned before, young children whose faces are on a similar level to a dog's mouth can sometimes receive severe facial injuries if they continually hurt or tease a dog, either deliberately or unknowingly. The dog is usually blamed even if the child has provoked the attack. Appropriate education is our best preventive tool.

24 ANOTHER DOG IN THE FAMILY
– AGAIN NO PROBLEM

A. Introducing your new dog

You have made the big decision to add another friend and companion to your family. In most cases, your first dog will welcome another dog, especially if both of them are fairly young. On the other hand, an elderly dog often gets a new lease of life when a puppy comes into the home.

The question is often asked 'should I have two males, two females or one of either sex?' It is not particularly important provided the two are introduced and socialised correctly, although one of either sex is less likely to create friction. Two males or two females living together occasionally vie for position, especially when the younger one is fully grown and strong, and the older one becomes less physically able. This scenario is discussed in Problem 12D.

How should you go about the introductory process?

THE INTRODUCTION

1. Take your existing dog to meet the puppy when it is at the breeders if they will allow it.
2. The pup and older dog should meet on neutral ground such as a park prior to going home together into a restricted environment.
3. Give the older dog plenty of attention, but to begin with only when the pup is around, so that the puppy becomes associated with good things.
4. Start by feeding both of them in the same room, but space them out. Gradually bring the bowls closer together as feeding in close proximity will make the older dog feel that the pup is part of the family or pack.
5. The pup will have to be fed more frequently than the older dog, so we suggest you put the older dog outside *before* you put the pup's food down. Alternatively feed the pup outside and leave the older dog inside on the occasions when the pup is being fed individually.
6. Continue your usual routine as much as practicable, including taking both dogs out for walks. The pup will probably have to be carried part of the way so that it does not get too tired.
7. Provide a quiet area for the puppy to rest in and, by the same token, make sure that the older dog gets a break from the exuberance of youth!
8. Supervise their interactions for as long as you feel necessary to make sure that neither dog becomes stressed.

B. The visiting dog

Your friend has a dog and you want to visit each other's homes. How should you go about it if the dogs have never met before?

The method is similar to introducing a second dog into your home.

1. Introduce the dogs on neutral ground such as a park first of all. This is much less likely to create friction than taking one dog into another dog's 'territory'.

2. Once they have become acquainted, you can then meet in a more restricted area such as a garden.

3. Progress to the point where the dogs can go inside the house together. Make sure that you don't create a stress situation by taking the dogs into an area where they feel as if they cannot 'escape' from one another, e.g. passing each other in a doorway.

4. You can accelerate the dogs' acceptance of one another by teaching each dog to sit in front of you individually and then signalling them both to sit in that position and reinforcing them for doing so (Problem 12D).

5. If one dog is obviously 'superior' to the other, make sure you acknowledge their status by feeding the 'superior' one first.

NOTE: Some dogs, like some humans, will never be real friends! However, dogs that are well socialised will generally tolerate one another!

25 THE DOG AS A BURGLAR ALARM

– AN ASSET NOT A PROBLEM

Your dog's bark is probably your best burglar deterrent. Nowadays many people acquire a dog specifically as protection for themselves and their property.

Ironically, a wolf would make a poor protector or guard dog. David Mech, a wolf biologist of thirty years experience, studied a pack of wolves in the Arctic for a period of time over two consecutive years. He camped just a few metres from their den. Far from attacking him, he had to be careful not to scare the adult wolves into moving their cubs to another place.

Wolves have never developed the barking habit to any extent. They have few predators and barking would be counterproductive before or during a hunt. Some dogs which take on a distinct wolf-like appearance such as Alaskan Malamutes and Siberian Huskies also show little tendency to bark. The Basenji, the barkless dog of the Belgian Congo, is kept by many tribes to help with hunting. Its quietness helps it to catch prey as well as avoid predators.

Why then do dogs bark? There are numerous theories, but the one that seems to be the most widely accepted is that at some stage early man took a wolf cub home with him, perhaps as a playmate for his children. He found that a wolf which was confined was likely to make a barking type of noise at something, or someone, strange. This was valuable to him as warning of approaching enemies. Breeding from these wolves over a number of generations would have produced an increased tendency to bark.

Today most people expect their dog to earn its keep by barking a warning. This has become a double-edged sword! To the owner it is a source of protection, to the neighbours it is frequently a source of annoyance. According to a noise control survey conducted in New South Wales, Australia, barking dogs were reported as the number one environmental noise problem, with 24.6 per cent of people surveyed expressing concern. It outnumbered traffic noise by 3 per cent.

It is not necessary for a dog to be aggressive to be a good guard dog. The fact that people **think** that

they might be bitten is sufficient. However, the wealth of advertisements encouraging people to train their dogs to be guard or attack dogs makes many dog owners think that this is the proper thing to do. Frequently these dogs are taught by harassing and goading procedures which make them unnaturally aggressive. They can become very unpredictable and may attack without warning. Just lifting your hand to scratch your head may be perceived as a threat or signal to a dog which has been attack-trained.

It is a condemnation of our society that we actually create and promote aggression in another creature in an attempt to counteract aggression and dishonesty in man.

In recent times there have been a number of reported attacks on people by dogs which have been specifically bred for their aggression, for example Pit Bull Terrier types. When these events were shown on television we received a number of enquiries about where to acquire such dogs. Needless to say we were not helpful!

Authorities around the world are now adopting firmer attitudes towards the breeding, importation, training and owning of aggressive or guard dogs. Hopefully, in the near future they will be a thing of the past. There are so many different breeds of dogs to choose from, we certainly do not need to be producing dogs with abnormal temperaments.

The term 'guarding' is actually a misnomer as far as the *dog's* intentions are concerned! Let's look at a typical example of how the behaviour may be produced in the first place.

If we lived in a society where no one owned land and there were no fences so that everyone could come and go at will, humans and dogs would probably mingle with great confidence because they would be able to relate to each other naturally.

Set up fences and the scene changes. Many humans quickly lose confidence when they see a dog behind a fence. Their usual reaction is to back off and say something like 'good dog' in a quiet appeasing way.

THE *Bark on Signal* EXERCISE

Let us assume that your dog barks occasionally.

1. Place yourself beside your dog when it starts to bark.

2. When the dog barks, instantly give the voice signal 'speak' in conjunction with a small hand signal. This is usually a hand movement that mimics the opening of the dog's mouth as it barks.

'SPEAK'

3. Reinforce the dog.

4. Try to anticipate the next bark by watching your dog's body language. Give the voice and hand signal just *before* it barks.

5. Reinforce instantly when the dog barks.

6. Repeat points 4 and 5 on a few occasions until your dog becomes conditioned to your signals.

NOTE: It may be better for you to teach your dog to respond to a very subtle signal if you want it to bark on signal for protection. You could snap your fingers or scratch your ear or use any other gesture which the intruder won't recognise as a signal for your dog to bark.

Maintain your dog's response by reinforcing the behaviour intermittently.

The dog's initial reaction is to move forward boldly to investigate. It may then start barking because the human behaviour is unusual and the dog cannot understand it. It does not take many interactions of a similar nature to establish a pattern of canine responses which we mistakenly interpret as 'guarding'. In fact the dog was not deliberately protecting the property, it was simply responding to a stimulus in a dog-like manner.

Nevertheless, most owners like to feel that their dog can at least act the part of a guard. This can easily be achieved without teaching the dog to bite or become aggressive. We have already mentioned that the average person has a natural fear of injury and the thought of being bitten by a dog is very traumatic. The same cannot be said of electronic security devices!

Here are a few strategies you might consider to conjure up fear in the minds of potential intruders:

1. Place 'Beware of the Dog' signs at prominent parts of your boundary.

2. When someone unknown knocks at your door, take your dog by the collar and, as you open the door, say 'don't touch' 'leave' or 'guard', etc. A stranger is unlikely to test out your dog's temperament.

3. Speak to people in your locality or to children in the neighbourhood and pretend that you are having your dog attack-trained. It's amazing how quickly the word will get around. Of course, this won't work if you have a toy dog!

4. When you go out, leave your dog inside if possible. Criminals can always throw a bait to a dog which is outside in the garden and then gain entry to your property. It is more difficult for them to predict what your dog will do if it is inside the house and this will probably make them go and look elsewhere.

5. Last but not least, you can teach your dog to bark when you give it a specific signal (see page 129). This is particularly useful if you live alone, and hear or see something suspicious.

PROBLEM 26 HOW TO PREVENT AN UNWANTED PREGNANCY

Naturally the most obvious way to prevent pregnancy is to have your bitch spayed. However, if you don't want to do this for some reason, then you must be careful to avoid an unplanned litter. In Chapter 5 we discussed the natural hormonal phases which bitches pass through under the heading 'Sexual behaviour'. The signs of *pro-estrus* are fairly easy to see if your bitch lives inside the house, as you will notice spots of blood on the floor. If the bitch lives outside, then the early signs may not be so obvious and you will have to be on the alert for behavioural signs which indicate that she is preparing for mating.

She will tend to wander more widely when you go for a walk, visiting scent posts and urinating much more frequently than usual. Our own bitch deposits much smaller quantities of urine and does not squat down so low as she eliminates. She becomes less receptive to our signals and appears more introverted. These signs should alert you to look for obvious physical signs such as swelling of the vulva and the presence of a bloody exudate from her vagina which we have already mentioned. Fortunately for us, a bitch will not mate with a dog during this phase, so at least we have a few days' warning to put in place our preventive strategies. Unfortunately for us, if we have not realised that she is in season early enough, she may already have attracted the neighbourhood male dogs!

Ideally bitches in *pro-estrus* should be prevented from urinating or depositing vaginal secretions in the immediate vicinity of their home where other dogs can smell them. They should be taken to a park by car, walked under constant supervision and returned home by car. You will have to avoid entire male dogs in the park for obvious reasons. In this way, males in the neighbourhood will not realise that there is a bitch in season. Remember, her smell does not carry in the air for any distance. David trains many entire male dogs in our training area which is adjacent to our garden. Not one dog has shown the slightest awareness of our bitch's sexual readiness. An experienced stud dog might be a different proposition!

You will probably realise when your bitch actually comes into *estrus* and is ready to be mated. She will frequently moan and exhibit restless behaviour, flagging her tail to one side if any pressure is put on her rump. (Incidentally highly accurate tests are now available to pinpoint the actual day of ovulation for a breeder who is *planning* a litter.) Obviously she must not be allowed into contact with an entire male during this stage which usually lasts approximately nine days. If by chance, an entire male dog finds out that she is in season, then the bitch will have to be confined to the house or a secure pen, or as a last resort be temporarily housed in a boarding kennel. Some bitches will make every effort to reach a male and break through what has always seemed very secure fencing. You might like to have a few words with the owner of the male dog, if this is possible, as he should certainly not be out and about unattended! One male dog mooning over the fence may attract other dogs to gather there as well!

As your female passes into *met estrus* she will again become unwilling to 'stand' for a male and may snarl a warning if one tries to mount her. Don't take any chances!

She may show signs of pseudo pregnancy as discussed in Chapter 5: Sexual behaviour, and start to 'mother' objects such as slippers. This can lead to possessive aggression, see Problem 12E.

FRIENDS FOR LIFE

Exercises

For your convenience we are repeating some of the exercises which are constantly recommended in this book so that you can find them easily.

EXERCISE *1* **T**HE RECALL

INITIAL CONDITIONING

1. Wait until your dog is looking at you from a short distance away.

2. Move away from your dog to encourage it to come towards you, and drop your hand low to the ground. At this stage your hand should have food in it. You can use either your right or left hand, whichever is more comfortable, but usually the right hand is used.

3. Say, 'come', once only when your dog is actually moving towards you.

4. Reinforce your dog with the piece of food in your hand the moment it reaches you.

5. Remove your hand quickly away up to your waist level.

6. Repeat points 1–5 until the dog's behaviour becomes predictable, i.e. conditioned. This should not take more than a dozen repetitions.

Maintain conditioning. Once the dog's behaviour is predictable and it always comes to you on signal you should do the following to maintain its response:

1. Stop using food in the hand to help to stimulate a response.
2. The hand signal must remain the same whether there is food in the hand or not. Dogs can detect very subtle variations in hand signals.
3. It shouldn't be necessary to move away from your dog unless it is responding slowly.
4. The food which you are going to use as a reinforcer should be kept in a pocket or pouch where the dog cannot see it.
5. It is essential that you stop reinforcing your dog every time it responds correctly; however, do not make the intervals between reinforcers (the food) too long to begin with, e.g. reinforce the second, fifth, first, fourth or sixth response, choosing the quickest responses to reinforce.

Your reinforcement must become unpredictable so the dog does not know when it will be fed.
The difference between initial conditioning and maintaining conditioning should now be clear.

INITIAL CONDITIONING	MAINTAINING CONDITIONING
The Stimulus	
(a) Your movement away from the dog.	**(a)** Your hand signal low to the ground.
(b) Your hand signal low to the ground.	**(b)** Your verbal signal 'come'.
(c) Your verbal signal 'come'.	
(d) The food in your hand.	
	NOTE: No food to induce the response.
The Response	
The dog is *induced* to come in response to the above stimuli.	The dog *comes* in response to the above stimuli.
The Reinforcement	
The food given to the dog from your *hand*.	The food given to the dog **intermittently** from your *pocket*.

EXERCISE *2* **SIT AT SIDE**

INITIAL CONDITIONING

1. As your dog approaches you, turn your body so that your dog comes to your left-hand side and then bring your right hand, containing food, to a position in front of the dog's nose.

2. Raise your hand upwards in a flowing motion to approximately waist level *directly* above the dog's head.

3. Say 'sit', as soon as the dog starts to adopt the sit position.

4. Reinforce the dog immediately its bottom touches the ground.

5. Remove your hand quickly up to waist level.

6. Repeat points 1–5 until the dog's behaviour becomes predictable.

Maintain conditioning by eliminating food in your hand as a stimulus and reinforcing your dog intermittently with food from your pocket.

EXERCISE 3 THE SIT STAY

INITIAL CONDITIONING

1. Eliminate any distractions, especially moving objects.

2. Place your dog in the sit position at your left-hand side (Exercise 2).

3. Say the word 'stay', then step forward one pace with your right leg keeping the left leg static. Do not use a hand signal as this may encourage your dog to move forward.

4. Before the dog attempts to move, step back to your original position and give it a piece of food immediately.

5. Repeat points 3 and 4 a few times.

6. Gradually increase the distance you move away from your dog to two, three, four steps and so on.

7. When you can move about four steps away, turn round and face your dog, then return to it almost immediately. Give it a piece of food.

Your observation, timing and common sense should ensure good progress. You should never 'test' your dog by trying to advance too quickly. You and your dog must be successful at each stage of the exercise before moving on to the next. One extra step at a time in the stay exercise will bring about remarkable results in a very short time.

Introduce a visual hand signal as you say 'stay' when you are sure that your dog will not move from its position. It is usual to place your right hand in front of the dog's face. To maintain the response, reinforce the stay exercise intermittently once your dog has learnt the exercise.

EXERCISE *4* HEEL OFF LEAD

INITIAL CONDITIONING

This exercise requires excellent timing on the part of the handler. Unlike stationary exercises such as the 'sit', your dog will move with you into a constantly changing environment with all its distractions. In order to compete with these distractions you must give clear and meaningful signals and reinforce the dog when it is in the correct position close to your left leg. It may help if you begin to teach this exercise in a long, narrow passageway, using this environment to help you shape the right response. It is important, however, never to crowd the dog when you do this.

1. Start with your dog at your left-hand side. Carry several pieces of food in your left hand and a piece in your right hand. Both hands should be held at waist level.

2. Step off with your left leg, simultaneously sweeping your right hand forward parallel to your dog at its eye level.

3. As your dog moves forward say 'heel'.

4. Move your right hand back to waist level as you take three to four brisk paces.

5. After three to four paces, stop your dog by placing your right hand in front of its nose, and reinforce it instantly.

6. Take another piece of food in your right hand and repeat points 2–5 a number of times.

NOTE: It is most important that you reinforce your dog when it is close to your left leg, and not when it is lagging behind you or surging ahead.

Maintain conditioning in the usual way by eliminating food as a stimulus and gradually increase the heeling distance literally step by step. It is best if you give short enjoyable lessons measured by the distance covered rather than the amount of time spent in training. Three or four heeling routines, each of twenty to thirty paces, is ample. If you multiply this by three or four training sessions per week you will have walked more than 400 metres in the heeling position. Enough to make Rin Tin Tin look inadequate!

EXERCISE 5 **R**ETRIEVING

INITIAL CONDITIONING

1. Start with your dog near your left side. Throw an article about six paces away from you, making sure that it tumbles or bounces on landing to excite your dog's interest.

2. The moment your dog chases after the article, say the word 'fetch' and simultaneously move forward after it for a few paces.

3. When the dog has picked up the article, and not before, run away with your back to it thereby encouraging it to chase after you with the article in its mouth.

4. When the dog catches up with you, spin around quickly, dropping one hand, containing food, to its mouth, and putting the other hand under the article.

5. Say 'give' as the dog drops the article and reinforce it with a piece of food.

6. Repeat points 1–5 several times but not to a point where the dog appears bored.

7. Gradually increase the distance you throw the article.

Maintain conditioning by reinforcing your dog's response intermittently once the behaviour is predictable.

APPENDIX A YOUR DOG AND THE LAW

Copies of the Dog Act for your state or territory are available from the following sources:

AUSTRALIAN CAPITAL TERRITORY

Dog Control Act
Australian Government Printing Office,
CANBERRA 2600.

Enquiries re dog control legislation:
(06) 293 5188

NEW SOUTH WALES

Dog Act
Government Information Service, P.O. Box 258,
Regents Park, NSW 2143.
(02) 9743 7200

NORTHERN TERRITORY

Dog Act and Darwin City Council By-laws
Northern Territory Government Publications,
13 Smith St, DARWIN 5790.
(08) 8989 7152

QUEENSLAND

We were advised that Queensland does not have a
Dog Act. Dogs are controlled by local authorities
by way of ordinances.

SOUTH AUSTRALIA

Dog Control Act
State Government Information Centre,
25 Grenfell St, ADELAIDE 5000

Executive Officer, Dog Control, G.P.O. 1782,
ADELAIDE 5001
(08) 8216 7934

TASMANIA

Dog Control Act
Cruelty to Animals Prevention Act
Government Bookshop, 112 Liverpool St,
HOBART 7000.
(03) 6230 3289

VICTORIA

Domestic (Feral & Nuisance) Animals Act 1994
Information Victoria
Victorian Government Bookshop, 318 Little
Bourke St, MELBOURNE 3000.
(03) 9651 4100

WESTERN AUSTRALIA

Dog Act
State Print Publication Sales, 22 Station St,
WEMBLEY 6014.
(09) 383 8855

These Acts were under review in a number of states. We suggest that you stipulate that you want a copy
of the *latest* Act if you place an order. Phone numbers are correct to the end of 1996.
   Don't forget to check up on your local government by-laws as well.

UNITED KINGDOM

Dogs Act 1871 and Dangerous Dogs Act 1992
These are the most important acts for dog owners
to know about. There are also local by-laws in
many places. You can get information from: your
local library, the RSPCA and your council.

B WHAT KIND OF DOG IS THE EASIEST TO TRAIN?

Two of the more frequent questions we are asked are 'What is the most intelligent breed of dog?' and 'What type of dog is the easiest to train?'

It is often difficult for people to understand that a dog's ability to do things has more to do with its physical structure and temperament than with any inborn form of intelligence. Several thousands of dogs have come to us for training but we have not seen any complex reasoning ability in any one of them.

Dogs learn mainly by trial and error, repeating actions which are beneficial and avoiding actions which have resulted in nasty consequences in the past. They are not able to use tools, so their behaviours are limited to what they are physically capable of doing with their own body. They do not have a complex spoken language so they can't pass on information to each other verbally as people can. In short, dogs are not furry people!

Does this suggest that to see one dog is to see them all? Not really. Some dogs are better at jumping or agility, some excel at tracking, others are natural retrievers or diggers. However, relatively few dogs are good all-rounders.

In order for a dog to move fluidly into various positions such as the sit, stand and drop, its body and limbs must be in proportion and it must be free of problems such as hip dysplasia. Regrettably there are too many dogs that have been bred to achieve bizarre shapes which severely hamper their physical ability. Their brain is willing but their body is weak.

We have used the following criteria when assessing the trainability of various breeds. It must be stressed that this is our opinion based on observation and experience, and that we have no formal statistics to support our beliefs.

1. The dogs were trained with our particular method of training using positive reinforcement. It is *not* possible to assess a dog's true ability if it is subjected to force methods of training.
2. The dogs were physically sound and the tasks set were within their capabilities.
3. The dogs were temperamentally sound.

NOTE: Dogs which are nervous or fearful are not capable of learning to any extent, whether their fear is caused by genetic predisposition, lack of socialisation or harsh treatment. Fear overrides any other responses, see Chapter 7.

Provided the dogs in this group are physically and temperamentally sound, they are extremely easy to train

Australian Cattle Dog	Labrador
Australian Kelpie	Poodles
Border Collie	Rottweiler
Dobermann	Schnauzers
German Shepherd	Siberian Husky
German Shorthaired Pointer	Weimaraner
Golden Retriever	

Life is a game to these dogs. When their energy is directed meaningfully into training their responses are very good

Airedale	Hungarian Puli
Australian Terrier	Hungarian Vizsla
Collie	Jack Russell Terrier
Dalmatian	Old English Sheepdog

These dogs have an active and somewhat nervous or excitable nature which makes them easily distracted. When they are sufficiently motivated they train well

Bearded Collie
Bedlington Terrier
Belgian Shepherd
Bichon Frise
Brittany Spaniel
Cairn Terrier
Cavalier King Charles Spaniel

Cocker Spaniel
Fox Terrier
Gordon Setter
Irish Setter
Keeshond
Shetland Sheepdog
West Highland White Terrier

These large dogs try to respond like small dogs but their size inhibits quick reactions. What they lack in speed they make up for in reliability

Alaskan Malamute
Bernese Mountain Dog

Newfoundland
Rhodesian Ridgeback

At times they appear to have a one track mind, but with a little patience they train well

Basenji
Beagle

Chow Chow
Samoyed

Owners often feel pressured by the strength and vitality of these dogs. They are much more responsive to training than many people imagine

Boxer
Staffordshire Bull Terrier

Bull Terrier

Small dogs are often flighty and always seem to be in a hurry! That is just the way they train

Australian Silky Terrier
Chihuahua
Corgi
Maltese Terrier

Papillon
Pekinese
Pomeranian

The anatomy of these dogs slows or hinders their responses. They are not dogs you would choose to train in order to win an obedience trial. Basic training is fine for them

Basset Hound
British Bulldog
Bull Mastiff
Dachshund

Great Dane
Mastiff
Saint Bernard

These dogs are bred for speed and obedience training is not generally their forte. Their abilities lie in other areas such as lure coursing

Afghan Hound
Borzoi
Deerhound
Greyhound

Irish Wolfhound
Saluki
Whippet

Dog Training
The Gentle Modern Method
by David Weston

> *Enough to inspire any owner of a dog in need of training* - Ballarat Courier

> *Weston has done the world an invaluable service...he goes through the entire training schedule with more than a modicum of patience and commonsense* - The Courier-Mail

> *Simple, quick, effective and above all enjoyable for both trainer and dog* - Russell Mitten, School of Veterinary Science, Melbourne University

> *I strongly recommend this book to any dog or Hybrid owner desiring to teach basic manners and obedience* - Wolf Hybrid Times

The worldwide success that has changed the way we look at dogs in our society forever.

David Weston's book, packed with easily followed diagrams and photos, became an instant bestseller back in 1990. A couple of years, thousands of copies sold, and thousands of happy dog owners (and dogs!) later, his Gentle Modern Method is now widely accepted by even the most sceptical kennel clubs and breeders.

The reason? It works!

David Weston's revolutionary book is now available in editions across the English speaking world:

AUSTRALIA & NEW ZEALAND
Hyland House Publishing,
387–9 Clarendon Street,
South Melbourne, Victoria 3205

UNITED STATES & CANADA
Howell Book House,
A Simon & Schuster Macmillan Company,
1633 Broadway, New York, NY 10019

UNITED KINGDOM
Gazelle Book Services, Falcon House,
Queen Square, Lancaster LAI 1RN